U.S *22.95
CDN *28.95

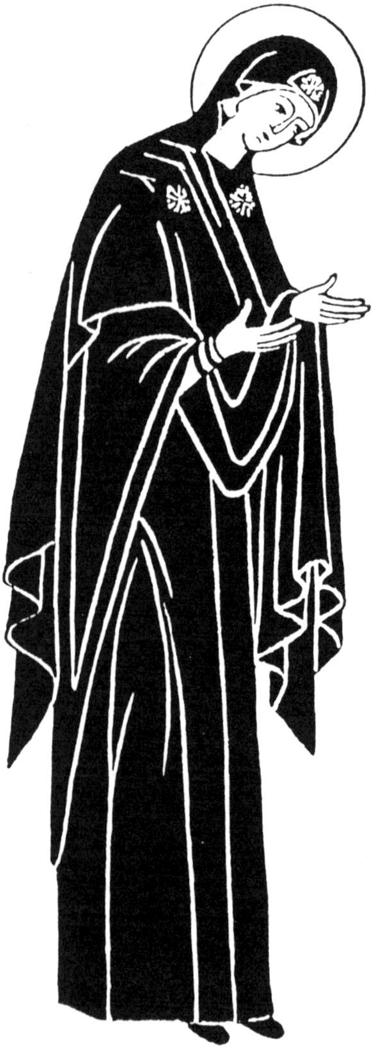

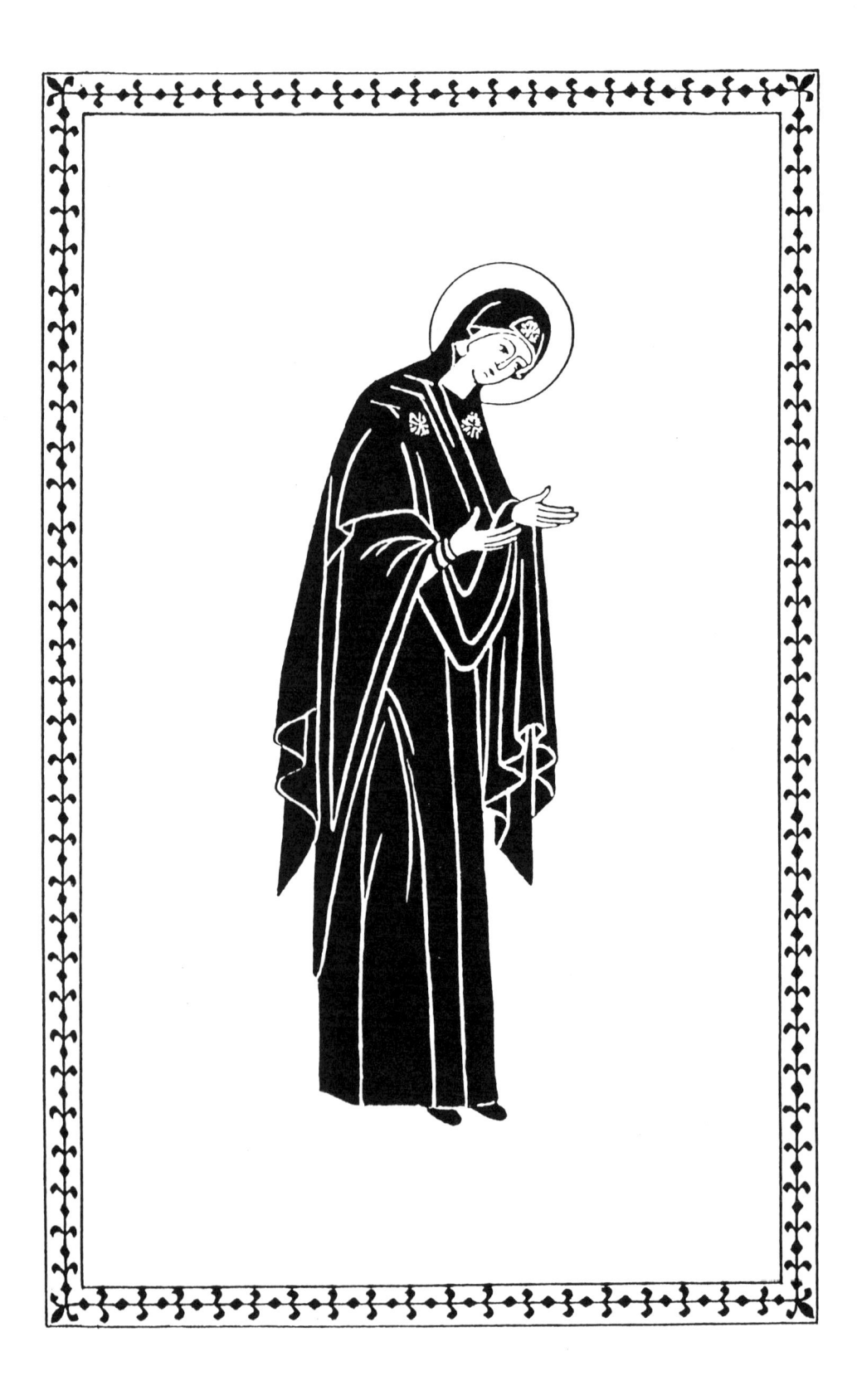

THEOTOKOS
Bearer of God

Mary, Mother of Our Lord God
and Saviour Jesus Christ

by

Joseph Raya
Archbishop

Madonna House Publications
Combermere, Ontario, Canada K0J 1l0

Copyright © 1995 by the author:
Most Reverend Joseph Raya

Publisher: Madonna House Publications
Combermere, Ontario
Canada K0J 1L0

Artwork: Marysia Kowalchyk
(Drawing on Cover and Endsheets from part of *Deisis*)

Canadian Cataloguing in Publication Data

Raya, Joseph M.
 THEOTOKOS:
 Mary Mother of Our Lord God
 and Saviour Jesus Christ

ISBN   0-921440-39-1   hardbound
ISBN   0-921440-40-5   paperback

1. Mary, Blessed Virgin, Saint. 2. Mary, Blessed Virgin, Saint—Theology. 3. Catholic Church—Byzantine rite—Doctrines. I. Title.

BT602.R39 1995   232.91   C95-900252-9

Acknowledgments

IN memory of my mother, Almaz-Mikhail Raya, and my sister Salma Raya, wife of Khalil Abu-Chahla, who taught me the infinite value and awesomeness of the female person reflected here in this book. "May her memory be eternal!" (as the prayer of the Church says.)

WITH humble and deep appreciation I acknowledge the collaboration of Doctor and father Deacon Robert Probert and his wife Lois in making this book; of Mary Davis, the agile and patient typist; and of Marysia Kowalchyk, artist and designer of the icon illustrations.

May they be blessed and well rewarded by the one whose life we tell and sing, the Bogoroditza, Mary, the Bearer of God.

Table of Contents

Acknowledgments v
Foreword x

PART ONE
MARY OUR LADY THE THEOTOKOS
IN HOLY SCRIPTURES

1. **Mary the Theotokos** 3
   Theotokos: Glorious Mother 4
   Council of Ephesus (431 A.D.) 5
   Special Motherhood 8
   Mary: True Mother 9
   More Mother than any Mother 11

2. **Mary the Virgin** 17
   Miraculous Conception of Christ 17
   Virginity and Human Relationship 18
   Virginity is Perfect Freedom 19
   Virginity is a Glory 20
   Virginity in the Gospels 23
   Virginity in the Holy Book of Islam 24
   Mary's Virginity, a Delicate Subject 26

3. **Mary Virgin and Mother** 27
   Stage 1: Conception of Christ 27
   Icon of the Sign 28
   Stage 2: Life in the Womb—God in our Human Flesh . . 30
   Stage 3: Birth-Giving 33
   Icon of the Birth-Giving 37

	Glorification of Mary's Maternity	38
	Feast of Mary's Motherhood: More than Birth-Giving	40
4.	**Divine Motherhood of Mary**	41
	Motherhood is Knowing the Other	41
	Motherhood is Presence	43
	Motherhood is a Sharing	44
	Motherhood is Intercession	46
5.	**Icons of Mary the Theotokos, Bearer of God**	51
	Deisis: Intercession	51
	Hodigitria: The Way	52
	Eleousa: The Tender One	57
	Colours in the Icons of the Theotokos	58
	Babe: But Still Lord and God	58

PART TWO
EVENTS OF THE PRIVATE LIFE OF MARY
OUR LADY THE THEOTOKOS

Prologue: The Private Life of Mary in Tradition and Legend
The Importance of Private Events 61
Legends and Marvellous Tales 62

6. **First Event of the Private Life of Mary:**
   Her conception in Anne's Womb 65
   The Parents of Our Lady the Theotokos 66
   Theology of the Feast 67
       Cosmic Joy 67
       Salvation and Regeneration of Humanity 69
   Fulfilment of the Old Testament 71
       Eve: Type of Mary 72
       Ark of Noah–Ladder of Jacob–Burning Bush 73
   History of the Feast 74
       Original Sin in Western Theology 75
       Position of the Eastern Churches 76

7. **Second Event of the Private Life of Mary:**
   Her Nativity 81
   Feast of Joy for All 81
      Joy for the Parents 82
      Joy for Mary Herself 83
   The Name of Mary 85
   History of the Feast of the Nativity of Mary 87

8. **Third Event of the Private Life of Mary:**
   Her Entrance into the Temple or Presentation 91
   The Tale 91
   The Enchantment of Tales 92
   From the Tent of God to the Temple of God 93
   The Story of the Entrance of Mary into the Temple 95
   Education of Mary 99
   Icon of the Feast 100

9. **Fourth Event of the Private Life of Mary:**
   Her Dormition–Assumption 103
   History of the Feast 103
   Meaning of the Feast 110
      Divine Worth of the Human Person 111
   Liturgy of the Dormition-Assumption 114
      Destiny of the Human Body 115
      Paraclisis 116
      Beginning of the Liturgical Year 118
   Icon of the Dormition 120

PART THREE
THE ROLE OF OUR LADY THE MOST HOLY THEOTOKOS IN OUR CHRISTIAN LIFE

10. **The Role of Mary in our Christian Life** 123
    Mary in the Early Christian Community 123
    A History of Honouring our Lady 123
       In the Liturgy 124
       In Preaching 125

	In Pilgrimages and Lighting Candles 126
Special Signs of Devotion in the Western Church 127
Devotion to Mary in the Eastern Church 128
The Acathist Hymn 129
	Literary Composition of the Hymn 130
	First Part: Annunciation and Incarnation 132
		First Chant 132
		Fourth Chant 134
	Second Part: The Adoration of the Magi 134
		Twelfth Chant 134
	Third Part: Our Divinization 134
		Fifteenth Chant 134
		Eighteenth Chant 135
	Fourth Part: Mary, Guide to Christ 135
		Twenty-Third Chant 135
		Kontakion of the Incarnation 136
	Conclusion of the Whole Hymn 136
Epilogue 137

ILLUSTRATIONS

- *Theotokos* from *Deisis* ii
- Our Lady of Tenderness *(Eleousa)* 2
- The Nursing Mother 16
- Our Lady of the Sign 29
- Nativity of Christ 36
- *Theotokos* from *Deisis* 50
- Our Lady of the Way *(Hodigitria)* 53
- Our Lady of Tenderness *(Eleousa)* 56
- Nativity of Mary 80
- Presentation of Mary 90, 101
- The Dormition 121
- The Annunciation 133

Foreword

THE unique theme of the symphony of our Christian religion is the Lord Jesus Christ, true God of true God, who became man to return creation and humanity to their divine Source and Origin, God the Father. Mary is an accompaniment to this great theme. She is Theotokos, the Mother who offered her whole human personality, body, soul, and spirit, allowing God to inhabit her flesh and blood in order to be in immediate physical contact with His creation. She conceived him and gave him birth. She suckled Him, nourished Him, and taught Him how to be human. She is His mother, Theotokos. This is the awesome hymn which humanity will sing from here to eternity.

Consequently, her supereminent graces and her role in the salvation of the world are not favours granted to Mary arbitrarily, to set her apart from the rest of humanity. Rather, they are gifts related to her being truly the Mother of the Saviour Jesus Christ. Whatever we attribute to her comes from Christ and is only an accompaniment to his music. It is only at the side of her divine Son that Mary can preside over the destinies of the world. We ascribe to her supreme beauty, perfect holiness, grace and dignity. Even angels stand in awe before her.

How awesome it is that a human person has been brought so close to the divine Essence; the very God himself has dwelt in her womb and has become her Son. Because her flesh and blood became God's flesh and blood, we sing to her the most sublime hymns, and her mere breath becomes life-giving.

Mary the Theotokos is an object of admiration, being the paradigm of a perfect humanity redeemed and glorified in this life and in the life to come.

In the present book I have no intention to reveal personal insights. I seek in all humility the spirit that vivifies our "tradition." I accept it as real and true, I surrender to its inspiration and live by it. I do not quote references in their entirety, not because of distraction or unconcern, but because the Gospel and the Fathers have become my flesh and blood. I live by them. I breathe them as naturally as when they first were written down. In this book Church and humanity are going to sing and play the hymn of Christ who is the real and only Symphony of God.

Let us sing along. Let us sing this book with all its superlatives, repeated again and again: "glory," "radiance," "miraculous," "most wonderful, wonderful wonder(!!)," "more honourable than the angels," "more glorious than archangels," etc. All this flurry of words and expressions is only to say that what we are singing about is beyond our imagining, more powerful than our intellect, bigger and more real than our own comprehension. There is a flame in every truth that we affirm in our Christian faith which no human language can encompass or express without catching fire.

Mary is a woman of our human race. A real woman like all women. A real mother like my own. She has been sometimes represented in such a distorted way that we can hardly recognize her humanity. I am dwelling on her human reality combined with the glories of being mother, bearer of God.

Let us observe God playing the game of his infinite love in Mary and displaying his generosity to us by the divinization of our humanity in all its meaning and resplendent beauty. Let us join in His game and frolic in His delight.

+Archbishop Joseph M. Raya
Madonna House
Dormition of our Lady,
the Blessed Theotokos, 1994.

THE OPEN HORIZONS

WISHING in his supreme goodness
and wisdom
to effect the redemption of the world:

*When the fullness of time came,
God sent his Son, born of a woman, ...
that we might receive the adoption of sons.*
(Gal. 4:4)

*He, for us men, and for our salvation,
came down from heaven,
and was incarnate by the Holy Spirit
from the virgin Mary....*
(The Creed)

*At the message of the angel,
the Blessed Mother of God
received the Word of God
in her heart and in her body,
and gave Life to the world.
Hence she is acknowledged and honoured
as being truly the Mother of God the Redeemer.*
(Lumen Gentium, art. 53, Vatican II)

PART ONE

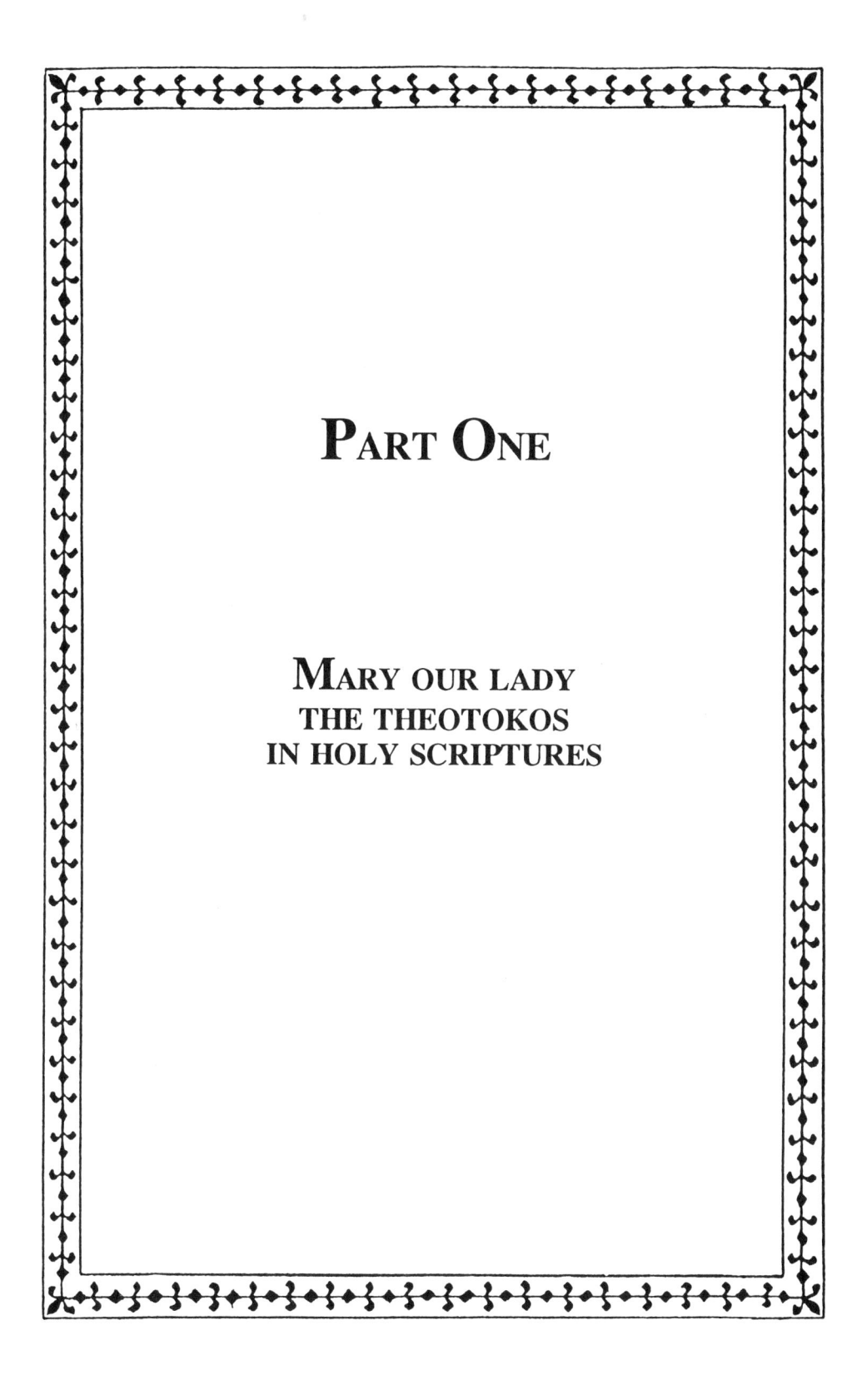

MARY OUR LADY THE THEOTOKOS IN HOLY SCRIPTURES

Our Lady of Tenderness
(Eleousa)

Chapter One

MARY THE THEOTOKOS

In Christian theology the divine motherhood of Mary, Theotokos, is more than an historical event. The word Theotokos contains the most solemn teaching of Christianity about the infinite Love of our God which was manifested in his Incarnation in the womb of Mary. In Incarnation, God became real man to identify with his creation, to save it, and to divinize humanity and the universe.

The word Theotokos is also a profession of faith in the royal dignity and divine worth of our humanity. It is indeed, from this humanity that God chose a girl, and drew her so close to his divinity as to make her his own mother on earth, a Theotokos. There is no greater dignity that can ever be bestowed upon humanity. Saint John of Damascus says, "The name Theotokos contains the whole history of the Divine Economy in the world and the whole mystery of the Incarnation (De fide Orth. III,2)."

"Divine Economy" means the plan of Redemption and of Divinization of humanity and of the universe, a mystery that existed hidden in God from all eternity and is now revealed in Jesus Christ, the God of God, and the Son of God who became man in the womb of Mary the Theotokos. Christ is the only living Sign and Manifestation of God in the world: "He who sees me, sees the Father (John 14:9)." He is the presence of God in the world. In him God came to abide with us. He is not simply the One who lived from conception to Resurrection. He is also all who preceded him in the history of humanity and all who will come after him. In him, therefore, there is the history of the revelation of salvation since Abraham. All the events and words of the Bible manifest God's intervention in the history of mankind and his great gift in the person of Christ. All the events and words in the life of Christ and what happened immediately after him in the New

Testament, in the Church and in the Sacraments, are signs of the presence of God in this world, and signs also of his presence in our lives. The essence of revelation is that God is in his creation as the Power of life for all of creation, especially for humanity.

THEOTOKOS: GLORIOUS MOTHER

THE word Theotokos is a Greek expression composed of two words: the first word *Theos* means God, and the word *tokos* means a woman carrier or bearer of a child in her womb. The expression Theotokos means that Mary is God Bearer, or Carrier of God in her own flesh to give him a human nature.

Being carrier of God in one's own flesh is the greatest and most sublime reality that can ever occur outside the inner circle of life in God. To be thus elevated to the edge of divinity is awesome and incalculably glorious. Being physically carrier of God in her flesh, Mary lives a miracle more miraculous than all the miracles that our mind can discover, invent, or express! All the other human attributes we ascribe to her, as those our liturgy repeats ceaselessly: "more honourable than the Cherubim," "more glorious beyond compare than the Seraphim," "sinless," "immaculate," "most holy," "most powerful," are only small gasps of fresh air we take in the presence of a spectacle larger than our imagining. The one who suckled and nourished God from her own flesh and blood is beyond all that human words can say. She is like a poem that stretches the boundaries of language to say what is somehow beyond saying; but we have to say it! Saying it changes the way we view God and think about him, about our world, and about ourselves. By saying it we also reflect afresh and understand better that which we have seen too often or too closely to be fully aware of. Our attitude in the presence of the Theotokos is the attitude of the artist and the mystic who can see the invisible, hear the impossible to be heard, and articulate previously silent or unheard voices and melodies. As God bearer, Mary of Nazareth is an object of admiration, of praise and joy, around whose personality we can weave marvellous tales and legends, and bathe in beauty.

Mary the Theotokos is the mother of Christ our King and our God, and the glory of humanity, particularly of all virgins and mothers.

The precise time when this expression was first applied to Mary has been difficult to establish. It is "confirmed" though by a unique piece of evidence in a papyrus fragment found in Egypt, dating from the third century, around the year 250. This papyrus contains a prayer which is the first recorded instance of a prayer to our Lady expressing belief in her divine motherhood (Theotokos) and her intercessory power. It has been adopted by the Western Church who called it the *Sub Tuum*:

Under Your protection we take refuge,
O Theotokos,
do not reject our supplications in our necessity,
But deliver us from danger....

The word Theotokos, applied to Mary, was also used by Alexander of Alexandria around the year 325, by the Council of Antioch in 341, and in general by the Fathers of the Eastern Church of the 4th century: Athanasius, Cyril of Jerusalem, and the three Cappadocians. It was formally sanctioned at the Council of Ephesus.

COUNCIL OF EPHESUS (431 A.D.)

THE Council of Ephesus was convened not to propose a dogma about Mary as some think, but to define and explain that the human nature of Christ which was taken from her was complete and real, and that this very nature was united *hypostatically*, which means substantially and totally, with the Divine Person of the Son of God. Thus, Christ is one person with two natures; He is fully human and fully Divine. Because Mary was the actual Mother of Jesus Christ, who was Son of God, second person of the Trinity, she was, consequently, really and truly Theotokos. Saint John of Damascus explains further that "the Word did not take his divinity from Mary, but the Word who had been with the Father from all eternity took flesh from her when the time of the Incarnation had come (De fide Orth. 3,12)." However, the primary purpose of the Council was to refute a heresy known as the Nestorian heresy.

It was probably on December 23, 428, that Produs, a famous preacher at Constantinople, and later its patriarch, delivered a sermon in honour of Mary in the presence of the newly installed

Patriarch, Nestorius. The conclusion of this sermon brought out some key aspects of the Incarnation. Produs declared:

Emmanuel has, indeed, opened the gate of nature,
because he was man;
But he did not break the seal of virginity,
because he was God.

As he had entered through the hearing,
so he went out of the womb.

He was born as he was conceived:
He had entered without passion;
He went forth in an ineffable manner.

The Prophet Ezechiel announced,
"The Lord God said to me,
'This door will be kept shut.
No one will open it or go through it,
since the Lord, the God of Israel,
has been through it.
And so it must be kept shut.

The prince himself, however, may sit there
to take his meal in the presence of the Lord'."
(Ez. 44:1-3)

And the preacher concluded, "Behold! This is an exact description of the holy Theotokos, Mary."

Nestorius considered this preaching heretical! For him, the union of the two natures in Christ, the divine nature and the human nature, was not physical and substantial but only moral. For him divinity did not really unite with humanity; there were rather two distinct persons in Christ—one was God the Word, the other Jesus the man. God and man were joined indeed but not united; or if united, they were joined only by a moral union. Mary was simply the Mother of the man Jesus, but not Mother of the Person God-made-Man Jesus Christ. Consequently, according to Nestorius, we cannot say that God really became flesh in Mary. There arose a serious controversy, which was wholly Christological, concerning Christ, and not concerned with a greater or lesser discourse on Mary.

Nestorius's teaching was immediately reported to the emperor and to the patriarchs of Antioch and of Alexandria. The latter, Cyril, composed treatises on the debated subject, and in 429 he sent them to the Emperor, to the Patriarch of Rome, Pope Celestine, and to John, Patriarch of Antioch, asking them to condemn Nestorius as he himself had done. John of Antioch wrote to Nestorius asking him to accept the teaching of the Church. Celestine convened a council in Rome which condemned Nestorius, and the Emperor called for a council to gather in Ephesus for the summer of 431. After careful study the Council made the final decision that Christ was of two natures, true God and true man, "hypostatically" united in the one and unique divine Person of Jesus Christ.

The final declaration of the Council is clear and reads like a song of triumph:

> *We confess and proclaim*
> *that our Lord Jesus Christ,*
> *the only-begotten of the Father,*
> *is real God and real man.*
> *He is composed of soul-reason and of body.*
>
> *In regard to his humanity,*
> *he was born of the Virgin Mary...*
> *For us and for our salvation he was born.*
>
> *He is consubstantial with the Father*
> *according to divinity;*
> *consubstantial with us*
> *according to humanity.*
>
> *The union of divinity and humanity*
> *was a real unity in him.*
> *Therefore, we recognize but One only Christ,*
> *One only Son, One only Lord.*
>
> *Because of this union without any confusion,*
> *we confess that the holy Virgin is Theotokos.*
>
> *God the Word was made flesh,*
> *he was made man.*
> *And he united to himself,*
> *since his conception,*

*the temple (our human nature)
which he assumed from her.*

*Mary is his Mother.
Therefore, she is Theotokos.*

Crowds of people roamed the streets of Ephesus that night with torches, wild with enthusiasm, shouting "Mary is Theotokos!"

SPECIAL MOTHERHOOD

"MARY is Theotokos" means that Mary is Bearer of God, in a real sense, as concretely as any human mother is bearer of her child. But Mary's motherhood is of a very special kind. With her, no human father shared the conception of her son. It was the Holy Spirit of God, the Third Person of the Blessed Trinity who overshadowed her and animated the seed of her womb, fashioning a perfect human nature which the divine person of the Son of God, the Second Person of the Blessed Trinity assumed and united to Himself, and thus became the Lord Jesus Christ, real God and real man.

Holy Scripture expresses this action of God in the conception by Mary of the Lord in an assertive, affirmative way. The annunciation of the Archangel Gabriel could not be more positive. He said to Mary, "You are to conceive and bear a son...." Proudly and unhesitatingly Mary refused the impossible dream, but when she understood that it was the will of God, she accepted. Then the Archangel closed the conversation by telling her, "The Holy Spirit shall come upon you and the power of the Most High will cover you with its shadow (Luke 1:35)." This last expression "cover you with its shadow" is used in the Old Testament for the bright cloud which was the sign of God's presence; and the phrase used by the Rabbis for marital union was precisely "to lay one's power over a woman." From this action of the Spirit, the Word, the Son of God became "flesh." The word flesh does not indicate simply a "body," but a real "human being." The Word became not only a human body but a soul also, with will, freedom, thought and speech, the whole structure—the whole of life and human sensibility, except sin. All these human realities became in Christ the manifestation and revelation of God.

Thus the Annunciation and the conception by Mary of the Lord have a spousal character which negates the presence of a human spouse. Mary will become a mother while remaining a virgin on the human side, and the power of her fecundity will be exclusively the work of God. Thus, Mary's is a very special type of Motherhood.

MARY: TRUE MOTHER

THIS special way of conception of our Lord by Mary did not result in a new person who had not existed before as is the case for all human persons. Mary simply offered a human nature to the Second Person of the Most Blessed Trinity who, as Person, has existed from all eternity, one God with the Father and the Spirit.[1] In Jesus Christ there is but one Person, the Second Person of the Blessed Trinity. It is this Person of the Son of God who took our human nature from Mary's flesh, and thus became Son of Mary, a real human being, while remaining perfectly God, one with the Father and the Holy Spirit. Christ has therefore two natures, human and divine, united in the one divine Person of his Godhead.

The Council of Chalcedon in the year 451 explains in a poetical and most solemn way the identity of Christ in his two natures, as God and as man. The proclamation of the Council was composed with expressions taken from all the different centres of theology in the Christian world, namely from Alexandria, from Antioch, from Constantinople and from Rome. Let us read with delight this declaration and feel one with the two thousand years of pure Christian tradition of both East and West on the reality of our Lord Jesus Christ, real God and real man:

Following the holy Fathers
we will with one voice

---

[1] In our near-Eastern languages the word "Mother" connotes a centre where the personality of a human being is formed—Christ's personality was not formed in any way by Mary. The expression "Mother of God", to the ear of the uninitiated, sounds blasphemous and an insult to God. Muslims and those who are not of our faith are horrified by it. Out of respect to their faith the Eastern Church avoids its use as much as possible, using instead the expression Theotokos, or Bearer of God, Walidat al Ilaah, Bogoroditsa!

*confess our Lord Jesus Christ
one and the same Son,
the same perfect in Godhead,
the same perfect in humanity,
truly God and truly man,
the same existing
of a reasonable soul and a body.*

*Of one substance with the Father
as touching the Godhead:
born from the virgin Mary, the Theotokos,
as touching humanity.*

*One and the same Christ,
Son, Lord, Only-Begotten,
to be acknowledged in two natures
    without confusion
    without change
    without division
    without separation.*

*The distinction of natures
being in no way abolished
because of the union,
but rather the characteristic property
of each nature being preserved
and concurring in one person*

*not as if Christ were parted
or divided into two persons
but one and the same Son
and only Begotten of God
Word, Lord, Jesus Christ.*

    The fact that no human father ever intervened to provide Mary with male seed to form Christ in her womb does not, in the least, derogate from the physical reality of her motherhood. When Mary completely accepted God's invitation to become bearer of his Only Begotten, her whole person became a flame of love that gave life to a new human being. The fire of the Holy Spirit overshadowed her, melting her whole self, body and soul and spirit, which she poured out to form a new human being.

MORE MOTHER THAN ANY MOTHER

THE question of the virginal conception of our Lord in the womb of Mary is so important that the Church has called upon drama, poetry and art to express its marvellous significance. She has not tried to "explain" its physical possibility or existence. She simply sings its wondrous reality.

Since Christ was to bring into this world something completely new, more creative, and more wonderful than anything in the history of mankind, namely redemption and divinization, he had to have his human origin only in a new and marvellous way. In him, humanity was to be recreated—it had to be a new humanity. Saint Paul creates a parallel between the first man, Adam, the earthly one, born of the earth, and the second man, Jesus Christ, the heavenly one, born of heaven. The first man, he tells us, is but a living soul; the second, the last Adam, will be himself a Life-Giving Spirit. "The first man being from the earth, is earthly by nature; the second man is from heaven, heavenly (1 Cor. 15:47)." Consequently, Christ's humanity had to be an entirely new creation, and completely the work of God alone.

According to Saint John those who are to inherit the Kingdom are, "born not of blood, nor of the will of the flesh, nor of the will of man, but of God (John 1:13)." Our Lord is first of all and above everything else the kingdom itself, "Son of God," our very God who, when he decided to become man, was conceived in the womb by the Life-Giving Spirit of God alone. This is the first assertion of the Creed which states, "he was conceived by the Holy Spirit."

The second assertion of the Creed, "born of the virgin Mary," defines the part taken by our humanity in the mystery of this Incarnation. The mention of Mary's role here is an affirmation that humanity accepted God's invitation and nothing more. In the name of humanity, Mary accepted the gift of God in her own flesh, saying: "Behold I am the handmaid of the Lord! Be it done to me according to Your will (Luke 1:38)."

The Creed affirms, therefore, two points. It affirms first, that the human nature of Christ owes its origin to Mary and to God alone, and not to any other human agency. The second point which the Creed affirms is that the only contribution of humanity to this event consisted in accepting the invitation of God. These two affirmations of the Creed are a clear profession of faith in the virginal Incarnation of God in the womb of Mary.

In her acceptance of the gift of God Mary became more mother than any mother because the humanity of her Son was completely derived from her own flesh and blood. In other words, Mary did not join some of her own female genes and qualities to those of another human being to fashion the humanity of her Son. The humanity of Christ was from his mother alone and from no other human source. The science of genetics has shown that every cell in a child's body contains the genes of both parents. The whole human nature of Christ was from his mother alone.

The motherhood of Mary resulting from God's action is a positive affirmation that she is more mother than any mother. It was God alone who initiated her motherhood by directly creating the life in her womb. In Mary's womb Christ remained perfect God, One of the Trinity, while assuming a perfect human nature. He is Son of the Virgin alone, exclusively hers in all that pertains to his humanity. Yet, in his divinity, he remains the Son of the Eternal Father, in no way diminished or absorbed by humanity. In Mary we see this marvellous union of divinity with our humanity. On the side of his humanity, the Offspring she bore belonged to her alone; on the side of his divinity, he belonged to the Trinity remaining "consubstantial with the Father and the Spirit."

The humanity of Christ is not merely a passive receptacle of God, a grace, a gift or a radiation of God's divine energy. It is deified to its very essence, one with the Godhead in the Second Person of the Blessed Trinity. He is God!!! It is Mary who offered her own flesh and wrapped God with it to make him visible, physically present and communicable to his Creation. This is awesome and most glorious for humanity, for Mary and for femininity.

From this doctrine we conclude that the indescribable intimacy which is positive in the flesh of Mary and fertile in the creative act of God is a unique sharing, a unique relationship. We dare use the expression that Mary is "Spouse of God," *Theonymphos*. Naturally we use this expression only in a whisper, and sparingly, because our carnal nature and human mentality are too preoccupied with a literal understanding of words. Such an expression could sound blasphemous to the uninitiated and weak in the faith. We must use it carefully, taking into account human limitation and deficiency in theological sophistication. The most important and exhilarating fact we can always boldly and loudly affirm about Mary is that she is the real mother of Jesus Christ who is our God, and more mother than any mother. There is no reality that can withstand the effulgence of glory of this unique reality.

We do not explain any further. Instead, we stand in admiration and silent awe whispering the hymn of the liturgy:

O Mother of God,
when it comes to singing
proper praise to you,
every tongue and language are at a loss.

Even supernatural intelligences
are rapt in wonder
when it comes to rendering honour to you.

But in your graciousness,
and because you know our holy longing
to sing your praise,
be pleased to accept our faith.

Intercessor of Christians,
we exalt you!
(Byzantine Daily Worship, p. 597)

Referring to Mary's physical conception of the Lord, the Byzantine Church uses many expressions to emphasize the complete absence of any male human involvement. We call her *Apeirogamos*—not destined to human marriage, *Apeirandros*—no man can ever claim her for a wife, *Anymfevtos*—without a spouse. Each one of these titles has a special connotation, but they all affirm one idea: that Mary was never united to a man in procreation, and that she was never meant to unite. This way of talking about Mary's conception of the Lord is not to demean marriage, or to imply that marriage was not noble enough, or holy enough, for Mary. It is rather a way to emphasize the real meaning and purpose of the Incarnation which is the beginning of a new humanity.

These negative terms may seem restrictive, but in fact, they are made to open our mind and imagination to visions of beauty and freedom in her who has experienced a personal love-relationship with God and had no need for further fulfilment with any human being. When Mary surrendered to the creative action of God, she must have experienced the fullness of satisfaction and the most perfect ecstasy possible to a human being on earth. No further physical pleasure, nor any other happiness from any human source would ever have added to that fullness. In the act of conception with the Lord, God "possessed" Mary and perfected her spiritually, psychologically, and physically with the fullness of everything that a woman can ever be.

Our God is a Blessed Trinity of three divine Persons, Father-Son-Spirit. Our Lord Jesus Christ is the second Person. He is God of God, of one substance with the Godhead as the Father and the Spirit. We believe that this second Person of the Trinity became real man who was conceived, born, and lived all the realities of any human being except sin. Mary is his mother, real mother, more mother yet than any other mother because she did not share the creation of his humanity with any human being. She is so real a mother that sometimes the Fathers of the Church delighted in describing her relationship with her God in terms of haunting sensuality. St. Cyril of Jerusalem writes:

> *O Theotokos*
> *thou didst stretch out thy right arm,*
> *thou didst take him and make him*
> *lie on thy left arm.*
>
> *Thou didst bend thy neck,*
> *and let thy hair fall over him....*
>
> *He stretched out his hand,*
> *He took thy breast and drew*
> *into his mouth the milk*
> *which was sweeter than manna.*
>
> *And he at whom the Seraphim*
> *could not gaze,*
> *and into whose face the angels*
> *were never able to look,*
> *did the holy virgin dandle in her hands,*
> *and she made bold without fear,*

and called him "My Son,"
and he called her also "My Mother."[2]

Thus Mary, the Theotokos, is the real and glorious mother of our Lord Jesus Christ!

---

[2] Discourse on the Theotokos. Miscellaneous Coptic texts in the dialect of Upper Egypt, ed. E.A.W. Budge, p. 701 ff.

The Nursing Mother

Chapter Two

MARY THE VIRGIN

MARY conceived the Lord *in a virginal way* which means without human intervention. She carried him in glory and honour for nine months because she knew with absolute certainty that her conception of him was from God. She gave him birth and remained a virgin because he was the Creator of all. The One, who, in the beginning, established the laws of human conception and birth, alters them now for his own conception and birth, combining in his Mother the two most splendid glories of womanhood, virginity and motherhood.

MIRACULOUS CONCEPTION OF CHRIST

GOD and his actions are marvellous. In Mary these marvels are experienced in a concrete way. In her, God transcends human logic, and his actions surpass the material limitations of the laws of nature. The one who made laws for the formation and development of human beings made for himself new laws more marvellous than the first. Questioning how God can act beyond the laws he has already established is to move in a cloud of blindness. It is like questioning God's power in creating this beautiful universe from nothing. To every why, whence, and how, we can only answer: here it is! He did it!

God is marvellous and his actions are dazzling miracles. In the first law of creation he determined that no woman is divine enough to combine virginity and motherhood; in the second, he made Mary, his Mother, sufficiently divine to combine both glories. In the first law, he determined that no human being can be born without the glorious union of man and woman; in the second, he willed his own conception in the womb to be a new kind of dazzling miracle, a union of himself with our humanity. God poured out his own glory upon Mary, and from his own glory overflowed the seed of a new human nature.

God is not confined to the limitations of our laws of physics and biology, as glorious and miraculous as they may be. He made them fixed, predictable, and possible to absorb even by our limited capacity for understanding. But when he willed to be involved in creating a new humanity he performed a new miracle which was more appropriate to his infinite and wondrous Being. God is the source of every reality even when this reality contradicts the present limitations of our human nature and overwhelms our understanding.

VIRGINITY AND HUMAN RELATIONSHIP

THE first laws God made for human conception are wondrous, ennobling, and divine. Human conception results from the most glorious action human beings can perform. Man and woman unite, offering to each other without reservation the pristine freshness of their beings. In this gift of each other they become an image of the Trinity which is an infinite and eternally present relationship of love, a *Perichoreisis* of God from Father, to Son, to Spirit, in a perfectly infinite unity.

A human person is indeed body, soul and spirit. The body is the physical organism, a structure of cells and energies forming part of the universe. Soul is the psychological make-up of the whole person, consisting in appetites, senses, feelings, imagination, reason and will. Body and soul together constitute the uniqueness of a person. Beyond these two elements there is also a third element, which Saint Paul calls *pneuma*, the spirit (Rom. 8:16). The spirit is the point of communion with the universe, the point of personal experience of the depth of our inner being by which we enter into communion with what is invisible. By the reciprocal offering of all these marvellous powers[3] of their beings,

---

[3] All these powers constitute the glory of the "Virgin". The word Virgin in Hebrew, as well as in most Oriental languages is *"Beit-ool"* which means the "dwelling place of God", his "house" where he is true and real. When this treasure house is communicated from one person to the other God becomes alive in a new form.

man and woman become richer, more human and, consequently, more intimately united with the divine.

Virginity is therefore the physical and moral fullness and integrity of all these powers. They constitute also spiritual virginity or the "seal of virginity." This is a state of being that combines the forces of body, soul and spirit in pristine freshness, keeping them vibrant in respectful readiness for surrender, awaiting the touch of the perfect lover. Seal of virginity is basically a thirst and a hunger for total identification with the Lover.

Mary did not have to surrender any of her powers to a human lover. She kept all her powers of body, soul, and spirit alive and vibrant to the touch of God to form in her the human nature of Jesus Christ. She kept "the seal of her virginity" in glory while at the same time receiving and accepting the seed that made her fertile.

In every icon that represents her, Mary displays three golden stars, symbolizing the eternal presence of this "seal of virginity" in her. On her forehead there is a star declaring the virginity in her body, which combines the freshness of virginity and motherhood: Mary is both virgin and mother. On her right shoulder shines another star, the symbol of the virginity of her soul: Mary was a virgin before motherhood. On the left shoulder there is also a star symbolizing her virginity after motherhood: Mary is a virgin in her spirit. Her virginity will last as long as her glorious motherhood, that is, for ever and ever. Mary is ever Virgin and a real mother.

Mary's virginal conception of the Lord is so luminous that one needs the language of angels to speak about it.

VIRGINITY IS PERFECT FREEDOM

FOR the Christian mentality virginity does not mean a mere physical integrity. It refers to personal freedom as well, to the capacity for union with God, or with the deserving lover. It is mostly an habitual attitude of complete readiness for love to be offered to the lover freely, joyously, and spontaneously. It is associated with those, who of their own free will, patiently guard the torrent of their love from bursting forth until they have found the perfect lover. This is the perfect freedom which liberates all the forces of the human person, transforming the person into transparency of body and soul, leaving him or her open only to the touch of the perfect lover. Freedom develops into effulgence of beauty, growing more luminous with every thought of the lover. And when this beauty is bestowed it becomes more than a royal gift. It is magnanimity.

No abuse nor any mere physical violence can by itself ever break the freshness of soul and spirit of a human person. The Lord said, "Do not be afraid of those who kill the body but cannot kill the soul; fear him rather who can destroy both body and soul in hell (Matthew 10:28)." For example, the scars of the nails forced upon Our Lord at the time of his crucifixion became to Thomas the means to identify him as "my Lord and my God (John 20:28)."

Our high regard and praises of virginity contain not the slightest censure of the goodness of the flesh, still less of the values of tenderness of heart. The goodness of the flesh and tenderness of heart exalt virginity because they represent the pristine wholeness of a person in body, soul and spirit. They contain a freedom of superhuman beauty radiating security and joy.

God did not force himself upon Mary nor darken her will to overpower her. He awakened her to freedom and gently asked for her consent. When human beings offer themselves to God they do not enrich him in any way. They simply allow him to enrich their gift and perfect it by completing in it his work of divinization.

Mary surrendered to God in all freedom and dignity, not to enrich him, but to be enriched by him and to open for him the way to descend to his creation and allow himself to manifest his infinite love for humanity.

VIRGINITY IS A GLORY

WHEN the Archangel Gabriel announced to Mary that she would conceive the Son of the "Most High," she hesitated. How could she do such a thing when she had no lover? "God it is!" said the archangel. It was only after she had been convinced by Gabriel that this would be the work of God alone, that Mary declared herself the handmaid of the Lord and surrendered in all gratitude and joy, because the proposed Lover was infinitely rich and totally present to her. He was the Giver and she the receiver. He was infinite generosity, exalting her and raising to supreme glory the exuberance of her vital forces. He tenderly "overshadowed her," not to take away but to give, not to be enriched but to enrich and make her virginity more glorious and her motherhood more meaningful.

The virginal motherhood in Mary expresses the most ineffable union between God and his creation, a union more intimate and more exhilarating than any human union or intimacy. God and woman meet in the Son who belongs equally to both, and Mary is the total woman, both virgin and mother.

With Saint Basil, humanity has been singing to her with amazed exultation:

> *In you, O woman full of grace,*
> *all creation exults.*
>
> *In you the hierarchy of angels,*
> *together with the human race rejoice.*
>
> *From you God took flesh.*
> *He made you a holy temple,*
> *a spiritual paradise*
> *and the glory of virgins.*
>
> *From you, our God,*
> *who is before eternity,*
> *become a Child!*
>
> *He has made your womb his throne*
> *making it more spacious*
> *than the heavens.*
>
> *In you, O Woman full of grace,*
> *all creation exults.*
>
> *Glory to you!*

Mary understood her own feminine dignity and grandeur so clearly that she proclaimed it in a fiery song of glory:

> *My whole being magnifies the Lord,*
> *My heart rejoices in God my Saviour.*
>   *O You higher in honour ...*

Because he has looked upon me, the little one,
all generations shall call me blessed.
    O You higher in honour ...

The Mighty himself has done in me great things,
Holy he is, and his faithfulness is forever.
    O You higher in honour ...

He has done marvellous deeds,
and scattered the proud in their conceit.
    O You higher in honour ...

He has put down the mighty from their thrones,
and has exalted the humble.
    O You higher in honour ...

He has filled the hungry with good things,
and the rich he has sent away empty.
    O You higher in honour ...

He has received Israel, his servant,
because his love is forever faithful.
    O You higher in honour ...

As he has said it to our Fathers:
to Abraham and to all generations. (Luke 1:46-55)
    O You higher in honour ....

The Church does not sing this hymn of the Theotokos in one continuous reading. She stops at every couplet to share in the joy of Mary and in the triumph of the universe in the Incarnation of our God, by saying:

O You higher in honour
than the Cherubim
And more glorious beyond compare
than the Seraphim,

You gave birth to God in virginity
You are truly Theotokos.
You we do exalt.

VIRGINITY IN THE GOSPELS

THE Gospels themselves are very clear about the virginity of Mary, but very delicately respectful in mentioning it. Luke expresses it in a whisper: "The angel of the Lord said to Mary: For the Holy Spirit shall come upon you, and the power of the Most High shall overshadow you. Therefore, the Holy One who shall be born of you shall be called Son of God (Luke 1:35)." With equal discretion Matthew too proclaims Mary a virgin: "Joseph, son of David, fear not to take unto you Mary, your spouse. For He who is conceived in her is of the Holy Spirit (Matthew 1:20)." Calmly and majestically, Luke again presents the same sublime reality: "Joseph went up from Galilee with Mary... who was with child (Luke 2:4-5)."

Saint Mark is respectfully silent. Fearing to create the least impression that our Lord was born in the ordinary way, he never mentions the name of Joseph. To the people of Nazareth who were wondering about the identity of the Lord he puts their question clearly in relation only to his mother: "Is not this the carpenter, the son of Mary (Mark 6:3)."

Some biblical scholars find in the Gospel of Saint John, who was the closest friend of our Lady, a clear affirmation of her virginal conception of the Lord. They propose to translate verses 12 and 13 of the first chapter of Saint John's Gospel to read:

> *God gave the power to become children of God,*
> *to those who believe in the name of him [our Lord]*
> *who was born not of bloodstreams,*
> *nor of the will of the flesh,*
> *nor of the will of a husband but of God.*
> *And the word became flesh .... (John 1:12-14)*[4]

What a delicate and clear vision the Gospels open to our hearts!

Joseph was considered by his contemporaries to be the responsible member of the family; thus he was called the father. They said, "This is the carpenter's son, surely (Math. 13:55)." "This is Joseph's son, surely (Luke 4:22)." This was the only way for the Mother and Child to be able to live in peace, and not be

---

[4] *The Mother of Jesus in the New Testament*, Rev. John McHugh, p. 125.

stoned to death according to the law of Moses. Who would have believed the astounding miracle if Mary had let it be known that her conception was of God? Joseph himself had trouble believing it. Later on, Mary herself referred to Joseph as "father" through respect and delicate attention towards him.

Only later did the Church learn that the Son of Mary was the Son of God, and our very God in the flesh. Only later would the human race know the whole story, and admire and praise Joseph the patient and humble man who was not the real father but the legal protector.

VIRGINITY IN THE HOLY BOOK OF ISLAM

THE Muslim holy books are also delicately attuned to the virginity of Mary. In the Koran there are three related passages of great beauty. Let me quote the one from the Surat of Al Omran (47, 45):

The angels said:

> *O Mary, God himself promises*
> *you a Word of himself*
> *whose name is Christ-Jesus,*
> *Son of Mary, a glorious One*
> *in the present world*
> *and in the world to come.*
>
> *He is one of the elect.*
> *He will teach humanity*
> *as a child and as a grown up man.*
> *He is holy—one of the holy ones.*

Mary answered and said to God:

> *O my God, how can I have a child,*
> *and no man has ever touched me?*

And God answered:

> *Is that so?*
> *God creates what he wants.*
> *If he ever decides on anything,*

*He says the word "Be"
and it is!*

The Hadeeth, the holiest book next to the Koran, reports the following story:

*Joseph, her guardian,
when he noticed her pregnancy,
could not contain the expression
of his surprise and suspicion.
He approached her with a series
of questions and said:*

*O Mary I have a question
I tried to contain and could not.
She answered—speak up!*

*He asked: can the wheat grow without seed?
She answered: certainly!*

*He asked: can the trees grow without water?
She answered: certainly!*

*She went on saying:
Don't you know that God made the wheat
without a first seed?
Can't he who created the tree
make it grow without water?*

*Joseph answered:
God is almighty!
He says a word
and things come to existence.*

*She asked again:
Don't you know that God created
Adam and Eve without a father or mother?
He answered:
Certainly!*

*Joseph realized that God has a special intervention
and did not ask any further questions,
because this was a mystery.*

> *He took care of her and he dedicated himself*
> *to the service of the temple with her.*
> *(Tabari 16, 43 - Rozi 5,53)*

MARY'S VIRGINITY, A DELICATE SUBJECT

OUR Christian religion is so delicately balanced that any inaccurate expression, word, or picture can distort its harmony. Mentioning the name of Joseph, for example, together with Mary and the Lord, or representing Joseph by the side of Mary or the Lord, could give a wrong message, especially to the uninitiated. That is why theology is very discrete about him, and Byzantine iconography does not represent him near Mary or near the divine Child.

The ever-radiant virginity of the mother of God has always been a glory for Christians, yet discussed very discretely and delicately, because, in Mary, virginity is not only a physical attribute but an inner spiritual attitude as well. Spiritual virginity lends significance and beauty to the physical; and Mary's physical virginity indicates wholeness and fullness. Virginity is basically a thirst and a hunger for total identification with the perfect Lover. The virgin preserves not only an inviolable self-possession but an unimpaired fullness of being which is irretrievably surrendered in the physical act which normal motherhood and fatherhood involves. The loss of virginity is associated, on the personal level with the sweet violence of a passion from which no human person could wish to feel himself or herself exempt. Yet it is still violence. With God, there never was violence. Thus, Mary was the perfect virgin and the perfect mother.[5]

---

[5] Idea inspired by Rev. Hopko.

Chapter Three

MARY VIRGIN AND MOTHER

THEOLOGY, iconography, and the liturgy view the maternity of Mary in three stages—conception, life in the womb, and birth-giving. Every one of these stages contains a special element, an extraordinary and miraculous intervention of God, in which our mind and imagination find unlimited wonder and amazement, and our joy and pride in being human find their fulfilment.

STAGE 1: CONCEPTION OF CHRIST

THE life of God in the womb was so miraculous that it was revealed to Isaiah the prophet in a glorious vision. In the year 734 before Christ, Isaiah assured King Ahaz of victory over his enemies if he remained faithful to God. To help the King's faith, Isaiah offered him a "sign," a miracle, as proof that he spoke in God's name:

> *The Lord himself shall give you a sign.*
> *Behold, a virgin shall conceive in the womb*
> *and shall bring forth a Son and you shall call his*
> *name Emmanuel. (Isaiah 7:14)*

This is Isaiah's vision of the Incarnation, a revelation of the Second Person of the Trinity dwelling in the womb. This is a prophecy of the life of the Son of God in the womb of a girl of our humanity. From all eternity, God has chosen Mary as the means of expressing his infinite Love. She is, then, the sign and the symbol of redeemed creation. As both a virgin and a mother, she is the unifying force making the world aware of the grandeur of spiritual and physical motherhood. Eve was the mother of all the living; she brought death by her falling. Mary is the mother of humanity; she brought life in its fullness. Because Mary is not only a mother but the Mother of our God she is more mother than any other mother. Hymns of glory are sung to her and an immense variety of icons portray her.

Icon of the Sign

The Church has always been sensitive to Mary as a sign and symbol of the re-creation of humanity. When the Word of God was made flesh in her, he not only became the head of a new humanity, but the Lord of a new creation. In his flesh, he embraced the whole of creation so that it might share in his divinity. In Jesus Christ dwelling in the womb, the universe was radically transformed; in his Person, the world was consecrated and sacramentally renewed: clay and stone, planet and animal, word and movement, everything was redeemed and renewed. Radiance of God! Song of beatitude!

A special type of icon called *Platitera* has been created to represent Mary as the Sign of the re-creation of the world. In this icon, Mary is enthroned in majesty worthy of her rank as Queen of the Universe and Mother of God. The divine Child is in front of her, facing us, with open arms. He is surrounded by a golden circle, a *nimbus*, the symbol of divinity, which shines brilliantly with light and divine glory. Our Lord is glorified beyond any earthly being, and his glory is reflected in every detail of his mother's features and attitude.

At times, Mary too is situated together with her Son in the nimbus. Since the human nature of the Lord is inseparable from that of his mother, so also his divine glory is inseparable from her. The difference between the God who is her Son and Mary the human mother is shown by means of colours and design. While the radiance of the Lord is of bright gold signifying divinity, that of Mary is bluish-green, pink and red, signifying a mere reflection of the divinity. The Acathist hymn expresses this truth by addressing Mary as the "fiery chariot who carries Christ-God." She is not salvation, but the "bearer of salvation"; She is not the Sun, but the "bright morning star that announces the Sun."

Our Lady of the Sign

The icon of the Sign is generally placed in the centre of the second tier of the icon-screen, the *iconostasis*, between the prophets, who advance toward Mary's throne in a procession-like movement, six on each side. They all carry in their hand a parchment on which is written what they have foretold about the coming of Christ. This icon of the Sign may also be placed in the centre of the apses as a *Platitera*—"The Virgin whose womb is larger than the heavens."

STAGE 2: LIFE IN THE WOMB
—GOD IN OUR HUMAN FLESH

THE life of God in the womb of Mary was as real as the life of any human being in the womb of its mother. Being really in the flesh and dwelling in the womb, God the Son is said to have "emptied himself." Indeed, God emptied himself of all the appearances of the glory and majesty of his divinity in order to appear in the form of our humanity. Who could have withstood or sustained the brilliance of his infinite being if he had appeared in divine glory? Saint Paul calls his appearance a *kenosis*. He wrote: "Jesus Christ being God, emptied himself and took upon himself the form of a servant, and was made in the likeness of men (Phil. 2:7)."

In order to emphasize further that his true majesty was hidden in our human form, Saint Paul uses a stronger word yet. He says that Christ took the form of a "slave," referring to his cross, to which only slaves were submitted.

The Gospels also recall that Christ was a descendant of David, consequently, a real member of our human family. To stress that his humanity was real the Gospels give two different genealogies of Christ both converging on Joseph, who appeared to his contemporaries to be the father of the divine Child.

On the two Sundays before Christmas, the Church celebrates the ancestors of Christ. The liturgy mentions Abel, Melchizedek, Moses and Aaron, and the prophet Elijah, and even Job, as having a connection with the humanity of Christ. These are not, properly speaking, ancestors, but they prefigured Christ, and some of them announced his coming. Their presence at the Feast of Bethlehem is to proclaim and stress the fact that Christ was one like them, a real perfectly human being.

Neither are the three holy children of Babylon true ancestors of Christ; yet they are celebrated and constantly mentioned in the hymnology of the Church, because their life in the fiery furnace is like a prophecy and a proclamation of Christ's real presence in the womb. As the flames of the furnace engulfed them but did not harm them, so the flame of divinity penetrated the whole being of Mary and dwelt in her, but did not consume her, did not diminish nor alter in any way her humanity, nor the humanity of Christ.

With this "cloud of witnesses" as Saint Paul calls them, on the Sunday following the birth of the Lord, the Church also celebrates Saint Joseph. With him she honours David, the glorious ancestor and King, and James, called "the brother of the Lord." All these remembrances and celebrations are to reassure humanity that the Child whom Mary was carrying for nine months in her womb was both "true God of true God," and also, a real man of our own flesh, solidly anchored in our humanity in every way, yet without sin. This *hypostatic union* of true God and real man, even in the womb of Mary is most evident in considering the difference between death as the inevitable result of original sin, and the death of the sinless One by His choice alone. Death was not imposed upon him as it is on all humanity. He himself chose to die in order to destroy death and make it a door to resurrection.

Through original sin, humanity had fallen into the curse of death and the servitude of sin. Every human being born of a woman was "subject to the curse of death." But God the Son, real man as he was, could not be touched by sin, or by the curse of death because of original sin. He was free of sin in the womb and he did not fall into any sin. Sin is incompatible with his Godhead. He carried all the sins of humanity in his flesh to destroy them. He assumed a sinful flesh while remaining the Holy Sinless One. He did not die as a punishment or as a curse for original sin. He chose to die to heal the curse of death. He willingly went to the cross and submitted himself to death in order to destroy death and obliterate its shame as a curse. Death could not overcome the Immortal One, for, as he himself declared:

> *The Father loves me, because I lay down my life that I may take it up again. No one takes it from me, but I lay it down of myself. I have the power to*

lay it down and I have the power to take it up again ....   (John 10:17-18).[6]

With a keen sense of humour the Fathers of the Church and the liturgy allude to the rage of the devil when he discovered that he who he thought was the "Slave," was really the "Master of all." They tell the story of how the devil tricked the first Adam into sin and death, and how the Second Adam, Our Lord, tricked him back by accepting death in order to defeat him completely and utterly destroy him. They describe how, when the devil grasped the body of the Lord, he thought that he had in his clutches another mortal one. Instead, he was overcome by the Immortal One. He brought into his kingdom the Saviour whom he thought to be a sinner, but he encountered the Sinless One who destroyed his kingdom forever. St. John Chrysostom expressed eloquently this so-called "trick" of our Lord and consequently, his victory over all the devil's might, over sin, and over death:

*On this day of the Resurrection
let no one fear death,
for the death of our Lord has set us free.
He has destroyed death by enduring it.
He has despoiled Hades by going down into its kingdom.
He has angered it by allowing it to taste of his flesh.*

*Hades is angered because frustrated,
it is angered because it has been mocked,
it is angered because it has been destroyed,
it is angered because it has been reduced to naught,
it is angered because it is now captive.*

*It seized a body, and lo!
it discovered God;
it seized earth, and behold!
it encountered heaven;*

---

[6] The original Creed of Nicea does not mention the word "die" for Christ. It states "he suffered and was buried". The liturgical books also always mention the death of the Lord as "willed", "accepted", "chosen", "assumed", in order to show that death is destroyed by him: "He destroyed death by his death and bestowed life upon those who lay in the tombs". Death was considered a curse and a punishment for original sin.

> *it seized the visible,*
> *and was overcome by the invisible.*
>
> *O death where is your sting?*
> *O Hades where is your victory?*
> *Christ is risen and you are abolished,*
> *Christ is risen and the demons are cast down,*
> *Christ is risen and the angels rejoice,*
> *Christ is risen and life is freed,*
> *Christ is risen and the tomb is emptied of the dead:*
> *for Christ, being risen from the dead,*
> *has become the Leader*
> *and Reviver of those who had fallen asleep.*
>
> *To Him be glory and power*
> *for ever and ever. Amen.*

Glorious victory over sin and death arose from the humble beginnings of life in the womb of Mary!

STAGE 3: BIRTH-GIVING

FINALLY, the maternity of Mary is celebrated in her birth-giving. The birth-giving of Mary was as miraculous as her conceiving, and as glorious as her carrying Christ for nine months. God the Word came out of her womb as he had entered it—in glory. As the sun rises and penetrates everything painlessly and without travail, so Christ came out of his mother's womb, a "Light to enlighten every human face in this world," a "Light of the world." Gregory of Nyssa exclaims:

> *O the wonder!*
> *The virgin becomes Mother and remains a virgin....*
>
> *The virginity does not prevent the childbirth,*
> *nor does the childbirth destroy the virginity.*
>
> *It was fitting that he who entered human life*
> *that it might have incorruption,*
> *should let incorruption begin with her*
> *who ministered to his birth....*

And Gregory goes on to say that this seems to have been foreshadowed by the vision of Moses:

> *Moses saw the fire kindle the bush,*
> *and the bush did not wither....*
> *As there the bush was kindled*
> *and did not burn,*
> *so also here the virgin brings forth the light,*
> *but is not corrupted. (Vita Moses)*

St. Jerome, the first biblical scholar in Christianity, declares:

> *Mary is mother and virgin,*
> *virgin before the birth,*
> *virgin after the birth.*
>
> *I am full of admiration!*
> *How was the Virginal One born from a Virgin?*
> *Do you want to know how he was born of the virgin,*
> *and after the birth the mother is still a virgin?*
> *The doors were closed and Jesus went in. [John 20:19]*
>
> *You do not know how this was done,*
> *and you attribute it to the power of God.*
> *Attribute it also to the power of God,*
> *that He was born of the virgin*
> *and that yet the virgin remained a virgin*
> *also after the birth.*

When the Lord came forth from the womb he did not in any way diminish the buoyancy and limpidity of the virginal feelings of his mother. Rather, he increased her pride and joy of life, and added freshness to the expression of her love. He also renewed the meaning of motherhood and transformed it into magnificence. To her virginal feelings he added those of motherhood. Mary was the perfect virgin and the perfect mother. The liturgy proclaims:

> *Today a great and wonderful event occurs:*
> *a virgin gives birth*
> *and yet remains perfectly virginal.*
>
> *The Word becomes a Child*
> *and yet is not separated from the Father!*

The all perfect God has become a Babe.
He was born without breaking the seal.
By his swaddling clothes
He has loosed the chains of sin.
By his birth as a Child
He has healed the pains and sorrows of Eve.

Nativity of Christ

Icon of the Birth-Giving

In the icon of the birth giving at Christmas, Mary occupies, naturally, the centre of attention. She represents the "recreation and renewal of mankind." She is the New Eve and the Cherubic throne where God reposes. Every detail in her attitude emphasizes both the human and the divine natures of her Son.

She is tired. She lies on a mattress of purple fringed with gold, as on a throne of glory. Her face is radiant, because she knows in her whole being that her virginity has not been disturbed and that, consequently, her Son is divine. Her whole being is a pure flame of love. She looks tired and drained, yet calm, in deep contemplation of what is happening around her. She is keeping everything in her heart (Luke 2:19).

Mary is lying down because she is exhausted with a lassitude that pours from her whole body. She needs the rest after the great pressures of expectation and waiting and the loss of physical energy. Her motherhood is real and not an illusion.

The absence of travail in Mary's birth-giving is a clear sign of her perfect consciousness of remaining a virgin. As the Son of God is begotten from the Father, a Super-Abundance of the substance of the Father, so he was born of his mother, a Super-Abundance of goodness and generosity. Saint John of Damascus sings to Mary:

> *You have conceived the Word*
> *without the operation of a human father.*
>
> *And without travail*
> *You became Mother of God, Mother of the Son,*
> *Who shone out of the Father.*
>
> *Therefore we proclaim you to be Theotokos.*

Virginity is a divine glory. Motherhood is also a glory surpassing all glories. No other woman on earth could ever combine their infinite vastness. No woman was divinized enough to contain them both at the same time in herself. Only Mary was able to, because she is Mother of God. She was the marvellous object of the "good pleasure," *evdokia,* of the Father who made the laws of the universe and who, for the sake of his glory, and to show his infinite love for his creation, made special laws for the Mother of his Son.

At this sight of Mary as the object of God's "good pleasure," the Christian heart cannot help but express pride and enthusiasm, and sing for joy a hymn of praise. This is the song we sing to her at Pentecost:

> *Hail, O you the Queen!*
> *Glory of virgins and mothers.*
>
> *Singing your praise is beyond the*
> *eloquence of the most cultured tongue,*
> *and the wonderful manner*
> *in which you gave birth to Christ*
> *throws every intelligence into amazement.*
>
> *Wherefore we the faithful*
> *magnify you with one accord.*

As we explained in Chapter Two, the glorious combination in Mary of motherhood and virginity is also depicted in all her icons by three stars—one on her forehead, one on her right shoulder, and one on her left shoulder. The ever-virginity of Mary is a leitmotif and a song of glory that pervades our life and devotion.

Our enthralment with the glory of these human attributes of Mary, virginity and motherhood, is an essential part of our celebration of the glory of the Son of God. The ultimate purpose of the Christian religion is not to teach things about God but to celebrate him; not to hand down information about Christ, but to glorify him in what he really is: Life, Love and Truth. In this beauty of Christ as a human being, our religion reveals also the real "stuff" of which the human person is made, within which we have to grow and develop. The glories of Christ are ours, and his infinite delight belongs to all of us.

GLORIFICATION OF MARY'S MATERNITY

FOR Christianity, truth is not a formula, but a Person, the divine Person of Jesus Christ who is a Message of joy. In him, doom and gloom have no foothold, no meaning. He is the Lover of every human being, the *Philanthropos*, full of surprises and goodness. Human beings are made in his image, and Mary is the most glorious of all human beings.

This teaching about Mary is best revealed in the hymn of the Acathist, or the "Song of Praises of the Theotokos":

> *The whole universe blesses you*
> *and sings your praise.*
>
> *In burning love we cry out:*
> *Rejoice, immaculate one!*
>
> *Rejoice, holy book in whom*
> *the Word Christ is written*
> *by the hand of the Father.*
>
> *O Mother of God, pray to him*
> *to write the names of your servants*
> *in the Book of life.*

The liturgy insists on the contrast between God who holds everything in his hands, sustains everything in existence, nourishes every living creature, and the Child held in the arms of his mother, nourished and sustained by her own flesh:

> *You carry him who carries the universe,*
> *and you give your breasts to feed Him*
> *Who gives nourishment to all.*

Another contrast is found in the Eternal who created time and space and now begins to live in time:

> *The virgin conceives!*
> *the eternal God is born!*
>
> *The birth is visible*
> *and what is accomplished is beyond nature.*
>
> *O awesome mystery!*
>
> *What we behold is indescribable,*
> *and what we see is beyond understanding.*
>
> *Blessed are you, immaculate Virgin*
> *daughter of Adam, made out of clay*
> *and yet Mother of God the Most High.*

There is a term often used for God: he is the Uncontainable One, *Achauristos*, the Infinite, the Immense, yet circumscribed in a womb which thus becomes "larger than the heavens":

> *From you, our God who is before eternity,*
> *became a child!*
>
> *He has made your womb His throne,*
> *making it more spacious*
> *than the heavens,*
>
> *In you, O woman full of grace,*
> *all creation exults.*
>
> *Glory to you!*

FEAST OF MARY'S MOTHERHOOD: MORE THAN BIRTH-GIVING

THE sixth Ecumenical Council, held at Constantinople in the year 691, reminded Christian people that the synaxis in honour of Mary celebrated the first day after Christmas was uniquely in honour of her motherhood, and not merely a congratulatory one for her safety after a successful birth-giving, as people used to do for all other women. Mary's birth-giving was safe and sure, without pain or travail. As her conception was a miracle of beauty where the Uncontainable Word of God became contained in the womb in a manner beyond understanding and beyond imagining, so was her birth-giving beyond human expressing. Gregory of Nyssa says that "just as the Son was given to us without a father, so also the Child was brought forth without childbirth (P.G. 44, 105 A,B)." Christ came out of her womb as painlessly and as naturally as light comes out of the sun.

When God acts upon us, he never takes away any beauty or any quality of our body or soul; he rather adds pride and joy to whatever we possess. When Christ our God came out of Mary's womb, he did not take away any of the glory of her virginity. He rather added beauty and pride to her beauty and virginity. The day after Christmas or the octave day of Christmas (in the West), we celebrate Mary as Mother of Christ and as our mother. We celebrate it also in honour of every mother of our humanity.

Chapter Four

DIVINE MOTHERHOOD OF MARY

MOTHERHOOD is both a knowledge of the person to whom a woman unites in order to conceive, and a presence to the child to whom she gives birth.

MOTHERHOOD IS KNOWING THE OTHER

SELF-SURRENDER and self-revelation to another, and the reciprocal acceptance in the act of procreation, is the deepest and most perfect way of knowing a person. Scripture and our Christian culture call this personal surrender and reciprocal revelation that unites man and woman for procreation a *knowing*. "Knowing a man" or "knowing a woman," is specifically a scriptural expression which signifies a perfect union of body and soul.

The sexual union that joins human persons for the sake of love and/or procreation is never merely a physical process. Indeed, it is much more. It involves body, soul, spirit, mind, feelings, and all the affections. The person who pours himself or herself out into the other is really present in the other in body and soul and spirit. Man inhabits woman, woman inhabits man. They dwell in each other and become forever present to each other. This is the self-revelation and self-surrender of one person to another. This self-revelation and self-surrender touches the depths of human consciousness, awakening the instinctive powers of the body, mind and soul and transforming the whole self into glory. The partners become a pure radiance that compenetrates and transforms the two into one. This is "knowing" a person; this is the deepest and most perfect knowledge, much deeper than the knowledge of any other experience which science or philosophy can impart.

When Mary completely surrendered to God, God revealed himself to her in all her physical senses of blood and nerves, and in her soul and heart. She became inhabited by God and totally alive to the experience of the ecstasy of the supreme love which God poured into her. Mary knew God more perfectly than any other human or angelic being can ever know him.

The craving for warmth and intimacy that every human being seeks, reached in her the apex of glory. Her body, soul and spirit, and every power of her being, became a flame, all vibrant with God. God, who is the fullness of warmth and security, sealed himself in her forever by his faithfulness and infinite generosity. God is inexhaustible. The ecstasy Mary experienced in him was a limitless source of beatitude, an abiding and ever-growing ecstasy rising from glory to glory. No further pleasure or joy could ever be added to her plenitude. Mary attained the beatitude of the Kingdom described by our Lord in the Gospel where, at the final resurrection, the blessed "neither marry nor are given in marriage, but are as angels of God in heaven (Matthew 22:30)."

After having experienced the glory of being possessed by God, Mary had no more hesitation or fear about her virginal pregnancy. God was her security. She could now face her contemporaries, the Law of Moses which prescribes that such a conception should be punished by stoning unto death, and even Joseph, the patient and discrete suitor.

In her enthusiasm she hastened to her cousin Elizabeth who was also with child in her old age by a miracle of God. When Elizabeth encountered a greater miracle than her own, she cried out to the young maiden, "How is it that I deserve to be visited by the mother of my Lord (Luke 1:43)."

After her astounding "knowledge" of God, and the acknowledgement of her pregnancy by wise old Elizabeth, Mary could not contain the exuberance of her feelings. Her pride became exultation, and she burst out into a song of glory in honour of her femininity and of the great deeds of God in her. No woman ever expressed with such ardour the splendour of being a woman. Even her frailty and humble condition became in her eyes a first step for the ascent to "thrones."

At the sight of the marvels of God in Mary, Saint John Chrysostom exclaims in admiration:

> *Nothing can be found among humanity*
> *like the Bearer of God, Mary.*

*Consider, O man, all creatures and see,
is there anything that can equal
in glory the holy God-bearer, Mary?*

*Go around the earth,
plumb the sea,
search through the air,
examine in spirit, heaven, .
consider all the visible
and invisible forces and tell me,
is there a wonder similar among all the creatures?*

*She alone miraculously conceived in her womb
the One whom all creatures
praise in fear and trembling.*

*Blessed are the women of this world
because they no longer labour under the curse.
She gave birth to a Child
through whom she surpasses all the angels in glory....*

MOTHERHOOD IS PRESENCE

BESIDES being "knowledge," motherhood is *presence*. Motherhood is a relationship between mother and child. It is an inwardness from which life springs. Mother and child are thus intimately united. Motherhood in Mary acquired an all-pervading presence of God. In her flesh there was a living and physical connection between the Creator and his creation. Heaven was joined permanently to earth and earth became heaven. God united himself to his creation, and creation became divine.

The son of God—God of God—became the Son of our humanity and a Brother to every human being. All the children of humanity became one with him, and real brothers and sisters of each other. The teaching of our Christian religion could be summarized in this sentence of Goethe, "Woman is the road to heaven." No other way exists for God to come down to the human race, or for the human race to ascend to God and to be united in one family. This is the source of the Church's teaching that Mary is the Mother of the whole human race.

Motherhood is more than the physical processes of conception and birth: the child is a part of the mother, always present to her, not only while in formation, but even beyond death. A child is always a part of the mother. We cannot think of the Lord without envisioning his Mother standing beside him. Christ was and will ever remain the Son of Mary; and Mary, for all eternity, will be the Mother of Christ. Whenever we place ourselves in the presence of her Son, our Lord and God, we encounter Mary the Mother; and whenever we need a human face to brighten our fearful heart in the presence of God, she is always there, beside him, to uphold us and strengthen our resolve. Mary is the mirror wherein we contemplate the Son, the door that leads us to his presence. Through her he came into the world, and through her the world will ascend to God.

It is most important to remember that Mary can only be understood in the perspective of Christ, and that it is an error to view Christ from the perspective of Mary. Christ is the gleaming Jewel contained in the setting which is Mary. "Our way to God is Mary" does not mean, therefore, that Christ is remote from us and that there is a natural gulf that Mary alone can bridge. Christ is the only source of our salvation. But Mary is his Mother, and the very first of humanity who, in a most sublime manner, accepted God's gift. When she accepted, all of humanity said "fiat" which means: "let it be done to me according to Your will." Together with her and under her leadership, we encounter Christ who is our only Salvation.

MOTHERHOOD IS A SHARING

BECAUSE she is more Mother to her Son than any mother, and because the humanity of her Son belongs to her exclusively, Mary is a *sharer* in the Redemption of her Son and an integral agent in our destiny.

The contrast between the human and the divine was harmonized in Mary. Her motherhood joined her intimately with the Redemption of mankind because her flesh was the very flesh by which Christ accomplished our Redemption. This position of Mary as sharer in our redemption is not opposed to, and does not invalidate or contradict the truth of our holy religion as expressed by St. Paul: "There is but one Mediator between the world and

God—Jesus Christ who surrendered himself as a ransom for all (1 Tim. 2:5-6)."

The Lord Jesus alone reconciled creation with the Father; he alone offered the sacrifice of our redemption; he alone could be our salvation and our intercessor before the Father. But it is equally certain that the body he offered on the cross, the body by which he saved humanity and became the sole Intercessor and Redeemer, is Mary's own flesh; so that we may say that Mary truly shares in his redemption and intercession.

In fullness of obedience, freedom and surrender, Mary offered to Christ the "matter" he used for our redemption, her own body and blood. As Man he received from her the flesh in which he lived, suffered and died, and which he offered for the salvation of creation. His supreme sacrifice was indeed of infinite value because it was the offering of the Person of the infinite God himself. It was sufficient in itself to redeem the universe from sin and restore humanity to divine life. Yet the body by which he redeemed us and opened to us the doors of heaven was that of Mary. It was her flesh in him that became the instrument of our redemption. Her sharing in our redemption is, therefore, strictly related to the Incarnation. Christ is Mary's Son, just as he is the "very goodness of God."

However unique Mary may be, and however all-embracing her role in the divine plan of salvation, the fact remains that everyone, including her, is redeemed. Mary, the Mother of God, stands first in the long line of the redeemed. In the ranks of the saved, she occupies a pre-eminent place.

The liturgy never tires of repeating that Mary is truly the Bearer of God, Theotokos. She is more closely united with the Word of God, her Son, than any other mother could possibly be with her own offspring. Christ our God received not just a part of his human nature from her as we have received ours from our mothers, but all of it. Consequently, her motherhood expresses better than anything else how the love of God has linked her to our destiny, and to our historical existence. In bearing in her own flesh the Son of God, Mary bore within her all humanity! And all humanity became the "Son of Mary" as well!

That is why we call her "our only hope," "our only salvation," "our unique helper," "our protectrice," and "our only mediatrix"—not in comparison with Christ but in relation to any other human or angelic power. In the prayer of the daily Office we say:

> *O gracious One,*
> *You protect all those*
> *who have recourse to your powerful arm.*
>
> *We sinners, who are bent down*
> *under the pressure of sins,*
> *We who are in dangers and tribulations,*
> *have no other mediatrix before God*
> *than you the Mother of the Most High.*
>
> *So we bow before you.*
> *Deliver your servants from all adversities.*

MOTHERHOOD IS INTERCESSION

MOTHERHOOD is, finally, *intercession*. The Byzantine Church expresses this intercession in almost every prayer she addresses to Mary. There is one prayer we sing every day in which we proclaim the intercession of Mary and delight in it. Even children know it by heart, and love to repeat it on all occasions:

> *O Never failing protection of Christians,*
> *and their ever-present intercessor*
> *before the Creator,*
> *despise not the petitions of us sinners*
> *who have recourse to you.*
>
> *But in your goodness*
> *do not tarry to run to our rescue*
> *we who cry to you with faith:*
>
> *O Theotokos, make haste to intercede.*
> *Be quick to make supplication*
> *for those who honour you.*

At all the hours of the Divine Office, and at the Holy and Divine Liturgy, we do not tire of repeating: "Save us through her prayers and intercessions." Mary mirrors the bounty, generosity, and marvellous love of God for us. She gives a human voice to the mercy of her Son and Lord. All that she is becomes for us a channel of divine grace. The perfect expression of such an intercession is found in complines composed by Paul the Cenobite:

> *O Lady, Bride of God,*
> *Virginal, pure, immaculate,*
> *blameless, without stain or disgrace,*
> *who through your birth-giving*
> *united God the Word with our human nature,*
> *and established a link*
> *between our fallen state*
> *and the things of heaven....*
>
> *With the power of your maternity,*
> *beg your Son, my Lord and my God,*
> *that He open for me*
> *the depths of His divine kindness....*
>
> *O you who are compassionate,*
> *be my constant companion.*
>
> *In this present life*
> *be with me as an intercessor*
> *as a powerful help to turn*
> *away the assaults of my enemies.*
> *and to guide me to salvation.*
>
> *At the hour of my death,*
> *be with me to embrace my poor soul*
> *and to keep away the dreadful*
> *sight of the wicked devils.*
>
> *On the terrible day of judgement,*
> *deliver me from eternal punishment*
> *and make me an heir*
> *of your Son's glory,*
> *through the grace and the love*
> *for every human person of your Son*
> *our Lord and Saviour*
> *Jesus Christ.*

All the liturgical books, with enthusiasm and confidence, use various terms to describe the intercession of Mary. We ask Mary; Mary asks for us; and together with all the saints and angels we ask the Lord of all for goodness, for remission of sins, for consolation, for protection and for final salvation. In solidarity we welcome Christ, accept him, receive him and pray to be one with him. Praying and interceding is a community action. Christians are never alone; we are the family of God. We are loved, accompanied and surrounded by love. This is the Communion of Saints. Christians on earth belong to the ranks of angels and saints of heaven. The Christian runs to Mary, to the saints, to the angels, and to every other human being who cares, and together, in unison, we all run to the mercy of Christ.

Mary is the leader and choreographer, the officially recognized "intercessor," the "ambassador," the "legate," the "duly appointed and legally authorized" *presbia* to speak to God in the name of all humanity, and to humanity in the name of God. In the presence of God she is in a state of perpetual adoration and constant intercession for all humanity. Through her and with her, humanity asks for the remission of sins, for consolation, and for protection of body and soul. When we pray for special favours we imagine her surrounded by saints, apostles, martyrs and prophets. With her, we all pray for humanity to be "delivered from sin," from the disorder of "passion," from "anger," "hatred," and from "judging others." This is spiritual solidarity and "communion of saints."

This community prayer is beautifully expressed and often repeated in all our liturgies:

> *Let us remember our all holy, spotless,*
> *most highly blessed and glorious Lady,*
> *the Bearer of God and ever-virgin Mary,*
> *with all the saints,*
> *and let us commend ourselves,*
> *one another, and our whole life to Christ God.*
>
> ***To You, O Lord!***

Theotokos from **Deisis**

Chapter Five

ICONS OF MARY, THE THEOTOKOS, BEARER OF GOD

THE Church teaches that theology and liturgy do not suffice to express all the spiritual riches of our Christian religion—the messages of theology and liturgy must be completed by the praying art of the icon. The icon is not merely a representation of an event or of a person. The icon contains the whole theological message of Revelation in forms and colours. What the Holy scripture says in words, and what the liturgy sings and acts out in music and poetry, the icon "writes" in colours and human faces. The official term for creating icons is not "painting" but "writing." We "read" the icon as the artist has written it.

There are many icons describing various important events in the life of Mary and our Lord, and various roles and attributes of the Theotokos. Three of these are her roles of intercession (*Deisis*), leading the way to God (*Hodigitria*), and one of her most glorious aspects, her tenderness (*Eleousa*).

DEISIS: INTERCESSION

THERE are as many icons describing Mary's role of intercession as there are attitudes of praying. The general attitude of her perpetual prayer of intercession is represented in the icon called *Deisis*. The Mother of God, and John the Baptist, the greatest born of a woman, are the symbolic representatives of humanity. They both intercede for the salvation of the world.

In this icon, Christ our Lord is either seated on a throne shimmering with gold and precious gems, or standing in glory. At his right stands the Theotokos; on his left, John the Baptist. Both have an attitude of humility, and awesome surrender to the God of all. Mary holds both hands up to the Lord, carrying the needs of humanity and offering to him the Church and all generations to come. John is offering all the generations of the past and of the Old Testament which he represents in a special way. Sitting on a throne of glory Christ expresses majesty, fortitude, and a love that is continually pouring out goodness and salvation. When Christ is represented as crucified, the delicate features of his face are of a noble and kingly character, deeply compassionate, peaceful, and attentive to the voice of our supplication.

The icon of Deisis summarizes the doctrine of the unity of Creator and creation, and is its symbol. The faces of Mary and of John the Baptist are not the faces of specific individuals with definite personal characteristics. They represent every woman and every man. They represent humanity.

The movement of the neck of Christ indicates the strength with which God pours himself out upon humanity. In this expression of love, devoid of sentimentalism yet rich in intensity and in dramatic power, every detail is full of serenity and royal dignity.

HODIGITRIA: THE WAY

BEING always present to her Son, Mary is, in a special way, "Help of Christians," indeed, "Queen and protectress of the whole world." As representative of the mystical Body of Christ she leads the way to God—she is *Hodigitria*.

This role of Mary as Hodigitria is depicted in a series of icons also called "Leader of the Way." Mary is represented as holding Christ, her Son, on her left arm. With her right hand she points to him, inviting us to go to him as to the "Way." He declared himself to be the Way: "I am the Way, the Truth, and the Life (John 14:6)." Mary's gesture is one of tender humility and self-effacement, yet full of powerful assurance.

One of the most well-known icons of this type is "Our Lady of Perpetual Help," known also as "Salus Populi Romani." The original, from the seventh century, is in the church of Santa Maria in Rome. Mary and the divine Child are seated in majesty. In the upper left and right corners, angels hold, with awe and fear, the instruments of Christ's passion and death. The eyes of Mother and

Our Lady of the Way
(Hodigitria)

Son are filled with horror and sorrow, yet their attitude is calm and self-possessed. They seem to know the final outcome. The Mother is regal, the Son fearful, yet confident in his mother. Both his hands are placed on the hand of the Mother. She is the "shelter." She is greater than John the Baptist who confessed that he was "unworthy to stoop down and untie the shoes" of the Lord (Mark 1:7). In the icon, one shoe of the Lord is hanging loose; the other is tied. Mary has tied one and untied the other to indicate that she is greater than the Baptist.

Another type of Hodigitria is called *Platitera*, which means, "whose womb is greater than the heavens." The heavens cannot contain him who made them, but Mary's womb contained him. Mary is standing in majesty with open hands as if extending them to the ends of the universe. Her face is bright. Her eyes sparkle with a heavenly light of glory unequalled in any other representation of a human face. She is conscious of her queenship—she is the "Mother of the King of all." Her Son is the Creator and Possessor of all. He stands in her bosom as part of her very being, yet offered and surrendered by his mother to any one who seeks him. He holds his right hand up high, calling for silence and attention to his Word written in the holy and divine book of the Gospels which he carries in his left hand.

It is said that a *hodigitria* still exists in the holiest shrine of Islam, in the Ka'ba of Mecca. Abou-el-Walid Ahmad Ibn Mohammad Al-Azraki, the famous Arab historian writes: "This icon was painted on the column standing by the entrance of the Ka'ba. On it is represented Issa, Son of Mary, (to both be glory). Issa stands in his mother's chest, leaning on her bosom...."

It is reported in Arab history that when Mohammad, the Prophet of Islam (peace upon him), conquered Mecca in 630 he ordered that all idols and pictures be completely removed from the Ka'ba. When the workers were destroying them, Mohammad himself covered the Hodigitria icon with both hands and saved it from destruction.

The icons of our Lady of Kazan and our Lady of Smolensk are two other types of Hodigitria, very popular with Americans. In Russia, each marriage was to be blessed with the icon of our Lady of Kazan, and each bride was supposed to carry a copy of it to her new house.

Every event of the life of Christ is awesomely written in the movements and colours of the icon with Mary at his side, ever attentive and ready. She is at his birth and on the road to Egypt. She takes him to the temple for the circumcision. She seeks and finds him when he is lost in the temple. She presides over his return to Nazareth where he submits to her maternal authority, "growing in age and wisdom before men and before God (Luke 2:39-40)." Finally, she is at his side during his suffering and death, and she witnessed his resurrection and his ascension.

Our Lady of Tenderness
(Eleousa)

ELEOUSA: THE TENDER ONE

THERE is another type of icon that celebrates the human side of Mary's divine motherhood which is no less amazing and glorious.

Mary is represented as the "tender one"—*Eleousa* in Greek, *Hanouneh* in Melkite, and *Omeley* in Slavic. Her love is full of warmth and self-giving. In some icons of this type she is nursing her son. In a moving portrait full of power and mercy, such an icon illustrates a perfect tenderness—Mary is feeding the divine Babe who, in the words of our liturgy, "is grazing as a lamb at the breast of his mother." The God of all is being nursed and cuddled with infinite respect and love by a woman of our race. Mary "feeds the Creator of all." "She holds him who holds the universe in his hand."

In some other icons the tenderness of the mother is shown in the way she handles her son and looks at him. Mary combines both human and divine beauty. She envelops her Son with both arms, pressing him to her bosom. The Son surrenders with confidence. His hands embrace her, one hand wrapped around her neck and the other around her shoulder. He nestles up to her cheek. The face of the mother reflects the Son's divine majesty, and radiates glory and tenderness. Only the Son's powerful neck indicates that he is a perfectly formed man, and perfect God. He is dressed in a tunic and mantle, the vestments of adults, but the rest of his body is that of a child. There is perfect harmony between the perfect man, our God, and the Child of Mary. This icon is known also as the *Glykiphilousa* or "Virgin of the Sweet Embrace."

All newly-wed Melkite brides carry in their trousseau a *Hanouneh* to preside over the family's destiny.

The most well-known icon of this type among the American people is that of our Lady of Vladimir. The original icon was taken from Constantinople to Kiev, to the court of the Grand Duke, between 1120 and 1130. In 1153 it was moved to Vladimir, which is why it is called "Our Lady of Vladimir."

COLOURS IN THE ICONS OF THE THEOTOKOS

IN "reading" the icon of our Lady, the Theotokos, one has to pay attention to the colours often used in her outer garments, such as blue and purple.

The blue represents transcendence over all that is ordinary and merely material. Blue symbolizes fidelity and immortality, and inspires calm, tranquility, and security. It points to the heaven where God resides.

Blue is used mostly in the mantles of our Lord and in the robes of the Mother of God. The *porphyry,* or royal blue or purple, suggests richness and wealth, power and dedication. Royal blue is both regal and sacerdotal, used in olden times only by high dignitaries and priests.

In the Bible, Balthazar the King vests Daniel with purple because the latter deciphered the mysterious inscriptions on the wall of his palace (Daniel 5:7, 16-29). Jonathan, the high-priest and prince of Judea, the rich man of the parable of poor Lazarus (Luke 16:19), and the triumphant woman of Revelation (Rev. 17:4), are all vested in purple.

In the Byzantine empire only emperors wore purple. Those born in the "hall of porphyry" at the imperial palace were called *Porphyrogenitus.* The production of porphyry was also the monopoly of the imperial court.

Mary thus vested in blue and porphyry proclaims that she is the Queen, Mother of the King of all, the only High Priest and Saviour of mankind. Mary is our security in God, our hope and our protection.

BABE, BUT STILL LORD AND GOD

WE should never forget one final characteristic of the relation of Mary to her divine Son. The icons and the liturgy insist that Mary, in the consciousness of her motherhood, never loses sight of the divinity of her Son. The Office of Christmas is a magnificent example of this awesome attitude of Mary in the presence of the Lord. For her, as it should be for all of us, the Lord is primarily and above all Lord and God. To Kings, she proclaims that her Son is the King of Kings; to the Magi, she presents him as the Creator of the stars and the universe; to the shepherds, she offers him as the saviour of mankind. She invites all to "adore him in trembling and fear," as she does herself. And, when she sees him suspended on the Cross, she cries and proclaims:

My son, my senses are wounded
and my heart is burnt
As I see you dead!
Yet trusting in your resurrection,
I magnify you.

Whether in swaddling clothes in the manger, or on the cross, or sitting on a throne, Christ is "our Lord and our God," and not simply "Jesus." And the liturgy sings,

O cave be ready...
And you, O manger, receive the One
who wipes out all our sins.
Shepherds be alert, and witness
the awesome happening.
And you, Magi, who come from the East,
offer to the King your
gold, frankincense and myrrh.
For the Lord has appeared
from a virginal mother to whom his mother
bowed and adored as a servant,
And saying to the One who was in her womb,
"How were you planted in me,
and how were you formed,
You, my God and Saviour."

Thus, theology, liturgy, and iconography proclaim the glory of Mary, the Theotokos, as revealed in the Sacred Scriptures, and as granted out of the infinite love and generosity of our Lord and God.

Part Two

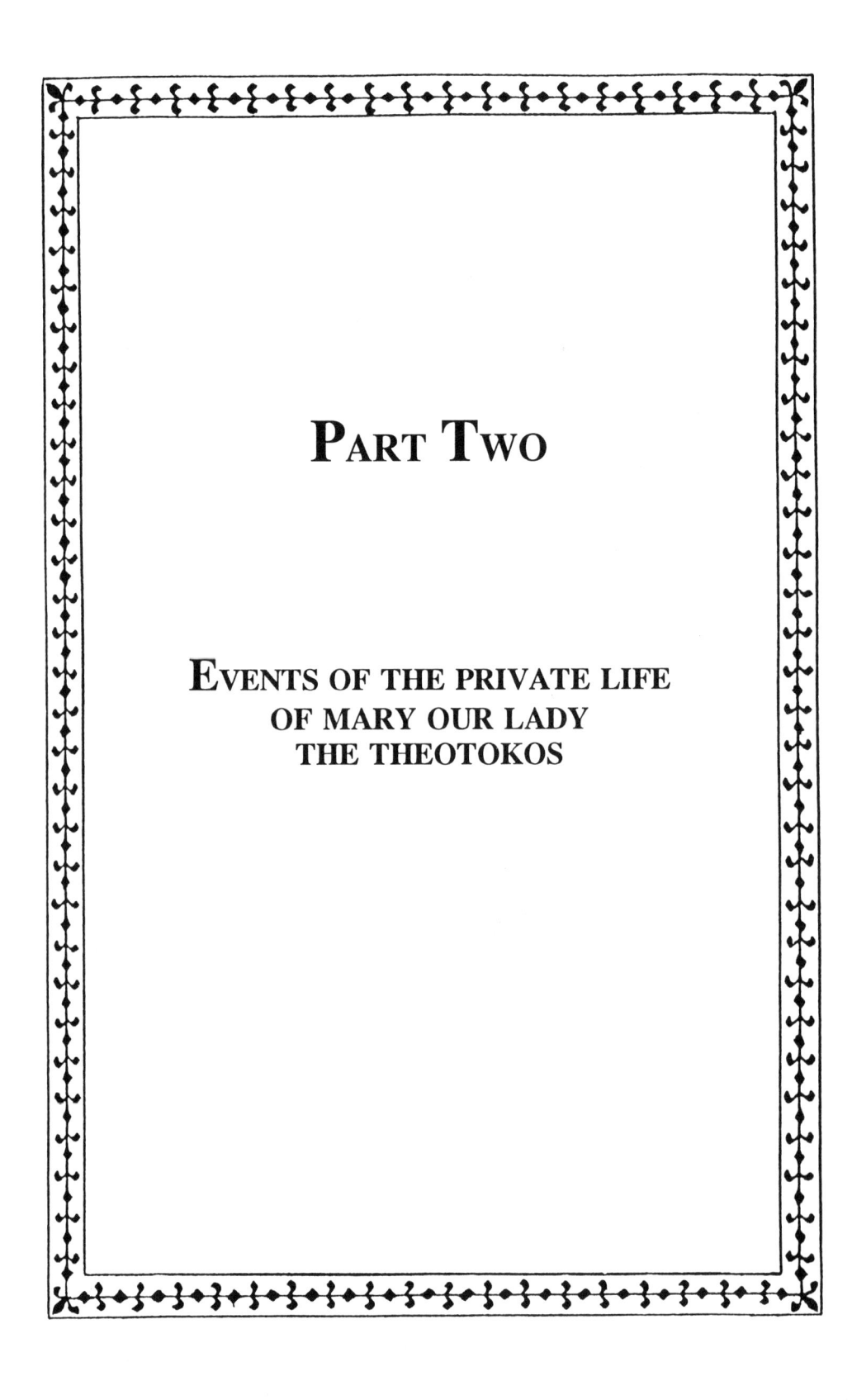

Events of the Private Life of Mary Our Lady the Theotokos

Prologue

THE PRIVATE LIFE OF MARY IN TRADITION AND LEGEND

THE IMPORTANCE OF PRIVATE EVENTS

THE events of the life of Mary, our Lady the Theotokos, are of two kinds.

Some are directly connected with our Lord, like the Annunciation, Christmas and the Presentation of our Lord into the temple. These events are reported in the holy and divine Gospel books and are part of Sacred Scripture.

Some other events like her birth, her growing up and her death are private happenings concerning her family and her contemporaries. They are not reported in Holy Scripture. They were remembered and kept in the private conversations of her family and friends and transmitted with care to successive generations.

For us Christians, Nazareth, Jerusalem, Bethlehem, Judea, and Galilee are not merely geographic locations. They are the home of the Lord, still inhabited by the memory of our God. There he moved around, he spoke, he loved and he died. Everything that he saw and every stone that he touched, every countryside, and every mountain and valley where he walked, and even the lake itself where he sailed are still vibrating with the echo of his voice and the warmth of his presence. They each have a soul that clings to our soul and forces it to love.

The apostles, the Baptist, the Magdalene, the sinners and the just who came in contact with our Christ, and every person, friend or foe, mentioned with his name are not for us ordinary people. They are persons with a special mystery, and a special relationship with him. Each one represents an aspect of his goodness, tenderness and generosity. Each one is dear to us and a member of a family to which we belong and which is ours.

Beyond all places and over all people who are mentioned in connection with Our Lord looms the majestic figure of his mother, Mary, the one who gave him his human nature and nourished him with her own flesh and blood. Holy Scripture does not mention much about her alone: when or where she was born, when or where she grew up, or where she finished her earthly life. Instead Holy Scripture includes what concerns our Lord and God in connection with Mary, his Mother. It is there wrapped in the majestic power of the inspiration of the Holy Spirit. What concerns Mary's private life belongs to her earthly family, to her contemporaries, and to humanity to be told in our human language and described according to our literary abilities.

LEGENDS AND MARVELLOUS TALES

HOLY Scripture's silence concerning Mary's private life teased the hearts and minds of early Christians. Christians eagerly collected the historical circumstances of her life, and whatever the elders could remember of past events of her family's history. They were afire with every detail they could collect to pass on to the generations to come. They garlanded events with luminous tales and wondrous circumstances befitting the human being whom God had prepared from all eternity to enter into the sphere of his life.

Naturally, once we have considered that God dwelt in Mary's womb, every detail of her life becomes an epic of great beauty, and we become composers and singers of sublime melodies.

At the sight of the Eternal in the arms of a girl of our human race, we become tellers of marvels worthy of the divine value with which God endowed his mother. It is enough for us to see him in her arms to become aflame with wondrous visions made of beauty and charm. We compose beautiful tales and enchanting stories of superb tones. The details might be from our imagination, but the spirit that inspires them is true, and God, who is their object, is the very Essence of every reality and of every truth imagined.

Legends and tales do not invalidate truth. They rather enhance its meaning and make it shine with brilliance. They generate a special warmth that creates and justifies in our own eyes the immense admiration and awe that we express in telling them.

Legends and history meet and fuse, and art is here verified. God is the Lord of angels and men, and the tales surrounding the events of his interventions in our human life have the same quality and degree of importance as the joy of primary truth.

In fact, at every major event of Mary's life all sorts of voices were heard, all kinds of stories were told. For her conception in the womb of her mother, they told of stars rising from the horizon and shining down on her parents' home. New types of music were born and new songs were sung in the universe. It was said that in the pitch dark of the night a glow as bright as the midday sun was shining around the house of Joachim and Anne.

Her birth was a festival of joy and of unsurpassed glory. Priests who were awaiting the salvation of their people sung songs never heard before, and choruses of archangels and angels danced around the Temple in glee.

Others told the story that when she was still an infant of three years she entered the Holy of Holies to be brought up and educated and served by archangels.

Others were ready to affirm that at her death they saw angels flying to all the corners of the world where the Apostles were preaching the Gospel. The angels gathered them on clouds, as on magic carpets, and flew them to Jerusalem to pay their last tributes to the Mother of their Master and Lord.

Christians told these stories, not with any intention to deceive, but because they realized that legends were symbols expressing a reality greater than our human imagining. These stories were told only to point to a bright mystery beyond the confines of our human comprehension. In them, God appears to be displaying with pride and joy the miracles of his love; and his people are so alive to his love that they respond with a love of their own.

Stories and legends are born out of the enchantment of love. They are necessary psychological tools to help dissolve our human attachment to the illusion that our present kind of existence is the only reality. They might be products of our imagination, but they emphasize that God is more real than our imagination and his care for our humanity far surpasses our human logic and expectations.

In God's Kingdom the presence of the greatest does not depress the small. Redeemed man is still man. Story and fantasy still go on, and should go on. 'The Gospel' has not abrogated legends; it has hallowed them, especially the 'happy ending'. The Christian has still to work, with mind as well as body, to suffer, hope, and die; but he may now perceive that all his bents and faculties have a purpose, which can be redeemed.[7]

Without stories we have no nation, culture, civilization, or true religion. The supreme expression of the human spirit is a story. The story is the most sacred possession, the way of justifying and sanctioning the values which are essential to the preservation of a community. It provides a concrete account of what is expected of humanity and what humanity expects of God both in this world, and in the mysterious darkness beyond death.

Admiration for the workings of God in Mary filled the heart and imagination of Christians, and was the constant delight of untold numbers of monks. Stirrings of amazement and delight ran through philosophers and theologians, through poets and artists, even through humble peasants, when they came to talk about the marvels God has worked in favour of his Mother.

The marvellous stories and beautiful legends Christians had collected about the life of Our Lady were recorded in special books called *apocrypha*. *Apocrypha* means "unauthenticated," or "historically uncertain," as opposed to Holy Scripture which is called "canonical," meaning "certain" and "authenticated." Saint James the lesser, also called "brother of the Lord," the first bishop of Jerusalem, is said to have written the first apocryphal book called the "proto-evangelium (or pro-Gospel) of St. James." In this book we find delightful details about the life of Mary's parents, Joachim and Anne, about Mary's birth, and about her entrance into the temple of God. In the *Apocrypha* there are also many marvellous details concerning her Dormition.

The first episode told in the pro-Gospel of Saint James is entitled the "Conception of Mary by Anne."

---

[7] *The Tolkien Reader*, Ballantine Books, New York, p. 73.

Chapter Six

FIRST EVENT OF THE PRIVATE LIFE OF MARY: HER CONCEPTION IN ANNE'S WOMB

In the Western Church since the year 1854, this feast is officially called the "Immaculate Conception." This title emphasizes the simple fact that Mary was conceived without original sin. This is the passive aspect of the feast—Mary has been conceived. Instead, in the East it is the active aspect of conception which is celebrated, namely Anne has conceived Mary. The feast is called "Conception of Mary the Most Holy Theotokos by Anne."

The anniversary date of the conception of Mary by Anne is the 9th of December, while her birth falls on the 8th of September. The time between conception and birth constitutes a period of nine months less one day. Our Lord's conception is on the twenty-fifth of March, and his birth on the twenty-fifth of December. For our Lord the period between these two events constitutes a perfect period of nine months to the day. The difference between the times spent in the womb is only a symbol to emphasize that Christ had a perfect humanity while Mary, even as Bearer of God, was not as perfect in her humanity as Christ her Son. The mentality of the ancients in the East related the perfection of our humanity to the time spent in the mother's womb. The more time in the womb, the more perfection our humanity acquires. Mary was not as perfect as our Lord was—her stay in the womb was shorter than that of our Lord.

John the Baptist was to be the witness to the Light, our Lord and God, a preacher of repentance, the voice of God crying in the desert, a prophet, and the baptizer of the Lord. The Gospel of Saint Luke tells us that his conception and birth were miraculous. John was to be so well connected with our Lord that God intervened in a special way to give his parents, Zechariah and

Elizabeth, power to conceive and have a child while they were old and sterile (Luke 1:5 ff). By comparison, the ancient Christians thought that Mary's conception and birth must have been more marvellous yet, and more glorious, even more miraculous than John's.

THE PARENTS OF OUR LADY THE THEOTOKOS

THE parents of Mary, Joachim and Anne, were known by their contemporaries to be God-fearing and faithful observers of the Law; yet they had not been blessed with children. Neither prayers nor tears helped relieve them from what was considered by the Israelites to be a curse and a rejection by God. To be without a child meant to be cut off from the memory of the generations to come and without any hope of giving birth to the Redeemer of Israel.

The pro-Gospel of St. James tells the story that one day as Joachim entered the temple to present an offering to the Lord, the high priest drove him away, reviling him cruelly because he was without an heir. Depressed and greatly humiliated by these reproaches, Joachim wandered into the desert to hide his shame. In his solitude, he opened his desolate heart to the Lord in a prayer of special fervour and despair.

Upon hearing of the humiliation inflicted upon her husband, his wife, Anne, went up to her garden to cry and pray also, saying:

> *O Lord,*
> *look down with pity upon me your servant,*
>   *and see my shame.*
> *To what shall I compare myself, O Lord?*
> *Shall I compare myself to the birds of the sky?*
> *No, they are better than I:*
> *You have blessed them with offspring,*
>   *and I have none.*
>
> *Shall I compare myself to the beasts of the earth?*
> *No, they are also more fortunate than I:*
> *You have also blessed them with offspring,*
>   *and I have none.*

> *Shall I compare myself to the fishes in this pond?*[8]
> *No, they have their young swimming about them,*
> *but I have no infant to fondle!*

While Joachim prayed in the desert and Anne in her garden, angels of the Lord appeared to both and announced to them the conception of a daughter who would have a great destiny. Overwhelmed with joy, Joachim hurried home with the happy tidings. At the "Golden Gate" of the city, he met Anne who was rushing to tell him the same joyous news.

THEOLOGY OF THE FEAST

THE Byzantine Church celebrates the feast of the conception by Anne of the most holy Theotokos in warm poetical expressions and theological clarity of thought as an epic of glory. In every hymn, and throughout the whole Canon of the day, words of rejoicing, clapping of hands, and dancing, are constantly repeated, inviting not only humanity but the whole universe to rejoice. It is a day of cosmic joy!.

Cosmic Joy

The primary invitation to joy goes naturally to the people of God who have been waiting for their salvation. The Office of the day proclaims:

> *The barren Anne leaped for joy*
> *when she conceived Mary the Virgin,*
> *who in turn will give birth in the flesh*
> *to God the Word.*
>
> *Overflowing with happiness, she cried out:*
> *Rejoice for me, O tribes of Israel,*
> *for I have conceived*
> *according to the will of God, my Benefactor,*

---

[8] The pond mentioned here exists to this day in Jerusalem; it is the pool of Bethesda, near the house of Joachim and Anne, the same pool where our Lord healed the paralytic. (N. Van der Vliet, *Marie ou elle est Nee*, Jerusalem, 1939).

> *who answered my prayer
> and wiped out my shame.*
>
> *According to his promise
> he has healed the pains of my heart
> through the pains of my birth giving.*

The hymnography of this feast proclaims that Anne's conception poured out great blessings upon the world. The salvation and regeneration of humanity becomes actual and the curse Eve had brought on humanity is healed and wiped out. Paradise is re-opened for all, and heaven united to earth. Divinization and transformation of the cosmos becomes a reality. The joy of the feast is truly a cosmic joy. The Office proclaims:

> *Today
> Rivers of graces flow in abundance.
> Rejoice, O heaven with the angels.*
>
> *Rejoice, O you the whole creation of God.
> Rejoice, humanity which has been
> divinized by the grace of Christ.*
> *(Office of the Day)*

At this universal rejoicing we look first to the Lord, the Author of the marvel, and we magnify him, saying:

> *I sing to your ineffable love
> for mankind, O Lord.*

And, looking back to the Mother of God in the womb of Anne, we recognize her to be already our queen and our security. She is our joy and glory. Even in the womb she carries the first announcement of the salvation of us all:

> *O my queen, you are my light!
> You are my glory
> and my guide to wisdom.*
>
> *You are my joy and my hope!
> You are for me a haven and my protection.*
> *(Office of the Day)*

In the liturgy of the day Mary is called "daughter of God." Naturally, she is first the daughter of Joachim and Anne, but because God prepared her and predestined her to be the mother of Christ, and because he gave her parents by a miracle a special power to conceive, she is called "daughter of God." From the very first moment of her life Mary was the object of the *evdokia*, the good pleasure of God. On the eve of the feast we sing with Patriarch Saint Germanus that the

> *glorious mystery, hidden from all eternity,*
> *unknown to angels and men,*
> *starts in the womb of Anne:*
> *It is Mary, the daughter of the Father.*

The Troparion of the feast is a perfect hymn formulating this mystery of God hidden from eternity and now revealed to humanity:

> *Today the bonds of barrenness are loosed.*
> *God has heard the prayers of Joachim and Anne:*
> *He has promised against all hope*
> *the birth of the maiden of God*
> *from whom the Infinite himself*
> *is to be born as a man,*
> *he who has ordered the angel to cry to her:*
>
> *Hail, O woman full of grace!*

The Kontakion sings:

> *Today the universe rejoices*
> *for Anne has conceived*
> *the one who is to give birth to the Word*
> *in a manner beyond all telling.*

Salvation and Regeneration of Humanity

The feast tells also of the "regeneration of humanity" because this conception is the fountainhead of our divinization and salvation. The dogmatic richness of the idea is sung in every page of the Canon. Here Mary is the one who will give our human nature to God. At the beginning of time, human nature and Creation came forth from the heart of God; in the future, the Son of Mary will divinize them both, and He will return them to their Source, the Heart of God. Because of Mary's conception in the womb of her mother, divinization appears to be near at hand and soon to be realized:

> *Today the human race received*
> *the first sign of its regeneration*
> *and the goodness of its divine adoption.*
>
> *Today the unshakeable Door of the Lord is conceived,*
> *and the all brightly lit City starts to glitter.*
>
> *The only one all immaculate is manifested*
> *by the angel to all the just*
> *who cry out with glee to the Creator:*
> *"a fruit is given to us, Mary,*
> *the source of immortality."*

And again:

> *Today a royal cloak of porphyry, Mary,*
> *is woven from the loins of David,*
> *and the mystical flower of Jesse*
> *is blooming!*
>
> *From it will come forth Christ our God,*
> *the Saviour of our souls.*

All through the Office of the feast there is a great explosion of joy in proclaiming that Mary *is* the fulfilment of all the promises of God. The longing of humanity to see his face and not die is also the final triumph of what God had barely initiated in the Old Testament. Mary *is* the joy and the glory of God. Joy and glory are expressed in the Office in hymns of supreme quality, which are unequalled in any other feast of saints, even that of John the Baptist. Even in the womb, Mary *is* the first of the human race saved and glorified by the life and death and resurrection of her Son, Christ our God, and this is supreme joy:

> *Today the great mystery that*
> *has been prepared from eternity, and*
> *whose depth angels and human beings cannot gauge,*
> *appears in the womb of Anne.*

*Mary, the maiden of God,
is prepared to be the dwelling of the King,
who will renew our human nature.*

FULFILMENT OF THE OLD TESTAMENT

IN addition to the doctrine of the regeneration of humanity and of creation, there is also, in the Conception of Mary in the womb, the idea of the fulfilment of the Old Testament's history. The Old Testament is, indeed, not only a book of the history of a people, but also a prefiguration of the spiritual history of the new humanity, and of how God had intended to renew it.

The Church has always taught several ways of understanding and interpreting the events and personages in the Bible. There is first the *literal* sense, where words and personages are taken with their obvious meaning. There is the *figurative* sense where words and personages admit of a growing understanding, emblematic or metaphorical. Finally, there is the *typical* sense in which persons and actions are directly signified, but they indirectly point to actions and persons to come in future times.

The English biblical scholar of the 20th century, Ronald Knox, summarizes this attitude of the Church in a few lines. After having remarked that in the Old Testament we find much that is violent and contrary to our Christian ideals, he says:

> *But through this tangled skein runs a single golden thread; between these soiled pages lies, now and again, a pressed flower that has lost neither its colour nor its sweetness. That thread, that flower, is the mention by type and analogue of her whom all generations of Christendom have called Blessed, the Virgin of virgins, the Queen of heaven, the holy Mother of God.... Our Lady is the culmination of that long process of salvation, of choosing here and there, and rejecting a human instrument unsuited to his purpose, which is so characteristic of God's dealing with his ancient people....* ("Esther as a Type of our Lady,"
> in Sheed's The Mary Book.)

We Christians weave beautiful poetry about Mary only for the reason that she conceived and gave birth in the flesh to our God!!! We recognize that there is no literal sense referring directly to Mary in the Old Testament, but we certainly can see her presence there in the typical sense. The dictum of the Fathers was:

The New Testament is hidden in the Old. And the Old Testament becomes manifest only in the New Testament.

Eve: Type of Mary

The first and most important type of Mary in the Old Testament is nowhere more evident than in the person of Eve. As Eve was the mother of old humanity, Mary is indeed the mother of the new—more brightly personifying innocence, holiness and freedom from sin (Gen.3:20).

As the second Eve, Mary has a distinctive function in God's design for our redemption. The discordant co-operation of the first Eve with the serpent and Satan in effecting our spiritual death contrasts with Mary's harmonious co-operation with God in effecting our return to grace. In fact, in the name of all humanity, Mary gave God her free consent, her co-operation and her unconditional acceptance of his invitation to become the Mother of his Son. Her surrender was complete. With eyes wide open and a will unfettered, she placed herself at God's disposal for the accomplishment of his plan of redemption. Eve was the mother of death and corruption. Mary became the mother of life and of divinization. Therefore, Mary *is* the "Second Eve!"

Gregory of Nyssa emphasized the comparison:

Woman was defended by woman.
The first opened the way to sin;
the present one served
to open the way to justice;

the former followed
the advice of the serpent,
the latter brought forth
the slayer of the serpent
and brought to light the Author of light;

the former introduced sin through the tree;
the latter brings in grace through the tree
of the cross. (Cant Canticorum, 13)

Ark of Noah–Ladder of Jacob–Burning Bush

By divine command, Noah built an ark in which he and his whole family escaped safe and sound from the common shipwreck of the whole world (Gen. 6:9ff). Through Mary's bearing the Son of God, the whole world was saved. The Ark of Noah is consequently a type of Mary. The ladder Jacob saw in a dream reaching from earth to heaven, and uniting heaven and earth is also a befitting symbol of Mary, the real "Ladder" that made heaven descend to earth and earth ascend to heaven (Gen.28:12). She is also called the "Burning Bush" which Moses saw on Mount Sinai. The presence of God was like a flaming fire burning on all sides around the dry bush without consuming it (Ex.3:2). It rather grew green and blossomed beautifully. So was Mary all filled with the fire of divinity, yet not consumed by it. The liturgy sings:

Behold!
The promises of the Prophets are realized,
for the holy mountain is planted in the womb,
the divine Ladder is set up,

The great Throne of the King is ready.
The place for the passage
of the Lord is prepared.

The dry Bush that fire cannot consume
is blossoming,
and the treasure-house of graces
is like an abundant flow of blessings
that heal the barrenness of Anne,
whom we glorify with faith.

Mary is also like the "Fleece" of Gideon that was soaked with morning dew on all sides while around it the land was parched dry; then again the fleece remained untouched by dew though the earth around was soaked (Judges 6:36-40). Mary is also the "Garden" enclosed on all sides, which could not be violated or corrupted by any deceitful plots (Cant. 4:12). Clearly, she is the

Root of Jesse: "There shall come forth a rod out of the root of Jesse, and a flower shall rise up out of his root... (Isaiah 11:1)." Mary is indeed, a descendent of the royal house of Jesse, and the sublime flower that rose from his root, although this is not specifically asserted by the evangelists.

Finally there are many other (Old Testament) types of Mary which seem to exalt her in her person and in her role as Mother and Queen. For example, she is "the house of holiness which eternal Wisdom built for herself (Prov. 9:1)."

Were these types intended as such by Almighty God? Surely this question never caused anxiety to our forefathers. Yet they did not hesitate to see in them a deliberate anticipation, on God's part, of the momentous role to be played by Mary.

Mary is called "divine" because she existed from the beginning of the world, in a special way, namely in the plan of God for the redemption of the world. We do believe that God had chosen her and predestined her from all eternity to be his own earthly Mother, and he delicately inserted her presence into every vision and in every pronouncement of the prophets. At her conception in the womb, great preparations were set up for her to become the dwelling place of all blessings and graces:

*Today rivers of blessings
flow upon creation.*

*O heaven, rejoice together with the angels!
O you creation of God, rejoice.*

*Rejoice, humanity, because you have
been divinized by the grace of God.*

HISTORY OF THE FEAST

THE event of the conception of Mary by Anne was celebrated in the Eastern Church on the 9th of December under the title of "Conception of Anne with Mary, the Most Holy Theotokos." The feast celebrates the marvellous intervention of God in favour of Joachim and Anne who, old and sterile as they were and dead to sexual relationship, became suddenly alive and strong enough to produce Mary. In the sixth century the feast grew in popularity throughout the whole Byzantine Empire and was adopted by all Eastern Churches.

The Western Church of Rome accepted the feast probably in the ninth century and celebrated it under the same title and on the same date. But when the concept of "Immaculate Conception" emerged in the Middle Ages, the title of the feast was changed in 1854 to become "Feast of the Immaculate Conception." This special title affirms that since the very moment of her conception Mary was free from "original sin."

Original Sin in Western Theology

In Western theology, "original sin" asserts that all human persons conceived of a man and a woman inherit in their very conception a human nature infected with sin, because of the Fall of Adam from whom the human race takes its origin. But Mary was, by a unique grace, preserved from this particular sin, inheriting a human nature in an untainted condition.

This teaching on Original Sin was first developed by Saint Augustine (354-430) of North Africa against Bishop Pelagius who was teaching that human persons can, on their own merits and powers, attain to salvation, and not necessarily only on the merits of Christ. For Augustine, on the contrary, every human person born of a man and a woman is born in a state of slavery to evil. For him, human nature inherited from Adam and Eve is, as he called it, *Massa damnata* which means a heap or a compressed mass of damnation. No one can be saved but by the merits of Christ which are obtained only through baptism.

In the teaching of later years Western theologians asserted that only Mary did not need baptism. She obtained the superabundance of grace and all holiness by anticipation, before Christ acquired them by his life and passion on the cross. Since her conception, Mary was without any sin, especially Original Sin. She was without a stain, or blemish, without a *macula*. She was *immaculata*!

All through the Middle Ages and until the nineteenth century, Western theologians were bitterly divided on this doctrine. Some with the Franciscan Duns Scotus (1308) defended it. Some others led by Saint Bernard (1140), followed by the Dominican school of Albert the Great and Saint Thomas Aquinas refused it. Their discussions were further complicated by the biological notion then prevalent, that the human soul is not infused into the foetus until 40 or 80 days after conception.

These same theologians were also handicapped by a lingering tendency to imagine original sin as a quality infecting the body even prior to the soul's advent.[9] The debate reached its peak of controversy during the reign of Pope Pius IX (1846-1878). In 1854 this Pope proclaimed the Immaculate Conception of Mary as a "dogma of faith." He explained it in these words:

> *The doctrine which holds that the most Blessed Virgin Mary was preserved from all stain of original sin in the first instant of her conception, by a singular grace and privilege of Almighty God, in consideration of the merits of Jesus Christ, Saviour of the human race, has been revealed by God and must therefore firmly and constantly be believed by all the faithful.*

After this declaration the Pope transferred the feast from the ninth of December to the eighth, and its official title became "Immaculate Conception."

This definition does not mean that Mary was conceived in the same way she herself conceived our Blessed Lord, namely without the intervention of an earthly father. Mary had, indeed, like all of us a father, Joachim, and a mother, Anne, and she was conceived by both of them. Immaculate Conception of Mary stresses the idea that when her father and mother conceived her, she was made sinless. She was not touched by "Original Sin."

Position of the Eastern Churches

The early Church Fathers regarded Mary as holy but not absolutely sinless. Origen and many Fathers taught that she had been imperfect like other human beings. But at the Council of Ephesus (431) when she was officially recognized to be "Theotokos, Bearer of God," she was declared to be:

---

[9] *New Catholic Encyclopedia*, Vol. VIII, p. 378 ff.

*All-holy, all pure,
higher in honour than the Cherubim
and more glorious beyond compare
than the Seraphim.*

No great issue was ever made in the East of the discussions the West was waging about "Original Sin." For the East, "original sin" involved the idea of a definite subjection of the human person to weakness, to the devil and in a special way to death as a curse and a punishment. There was no doubt among Byzantine as well as Latin theologians that Mary was indeed a mortal being who died our death even though sinless. Orthodox theologians refused the teaching on "Immaculate Conception" mainly because they considered it to be an arbitrary and one-sided decision imposed on all churches without any previous consultation and agreement on its real meaning, and the meaning of death as a punishment and a curse. The death of the Lord was not imposed on him. He "chose to die." He "accepted death." The Immortal One ascended to the cross to heal death and give it new meaning as a step to the Resurrection.

As for the purity and sinlessness of Mary, the Eastern Churches as a whole were proclaiming them to be essential characteristics of Mary. Mary was more than immaculate, and yet more glorious than all the angels of heaven. Saint John of Damascus is assertive on this subject. He declares about Mary's conception in the womb of her mother:

*O perfectly happy loins of Joachim,
from which has been ejected
an absolutely stainless sperm.*

*O glorious womb of Anne,
in which grew the "holy Babe"
by the gradual addition
received from her,
and after having been formed
was born, an altogether holy Babe!*[10]

---

[10] Sermo 2, P.G. 96, 664, B.

This means clearly that even the active conception of Mary in the womb of her mother was completely free from any contamination of sin, a view which could hardly have been accepted by early fathers in the West for the reason of the Augustinian doctrine that original sin is invariably transmitted by the sexual act. Besides all this, the Virgin Mary has always been qualified in Byzantine theology as *panamomos*, the perfectly stainless one. John Myendorff, the great Orthodox theologian, says that "Byzantine theology and hymnography do not cease praising Mary as fully prepared for the inhabitation of God in her womb. She was fully cleansed and sanctified." He quotes Sophronius of Jerusalem as saying:

> *Many Saints appeared before You*
> *but none was filled with grace as you....*
>
> *No one has been purified*
> *in advance as you have been.*

He quotes also Andrew of Crete (740) who is even more specific:

> *When the Mother of Him*
> *who is Beauty itself is born,*
> *[human] nature recovers in her person*
> *its ancient privileges,*
> *and is fashioned according*
> *to a perfect model*
> *truly worthy of God....*
>
> *In a word,*
> *The Transfiguration of our nature*
> *begins today.*

This theme is further developed by Nicholas Cabasilas in the fourteenth century:

> *Earth she is because*
> *she is from earth.*
>
> *But she is a new earth,*
> *since she derives in no way*
> *from her ancestors*
> *and has not inherited*
> *the old leaven.*

> *She is a new dough*
> *and has originated*
> *a new race.*

John Myendorff ends these quotations by saying that "the Mariological piety of the Byzantines would probably have led them to accept the dogma of the Immaculate Conception of Mary as it was defined in 1854 if only they had shared the Western doctrine of original sin."[11]

We can summarize the theology of the conception of Mary in the womb of Anne, her mother, in this paragraph from Vatican II:

> *The Blessed Virgin Mary was eternally predestined, in conjunction with the Incarnation of the divine Word, to be the Mother of God. By decree of divine Providence, she served on earth as the loving mother of the divine Redeemer, an associate of unique nobility.... She conceived, brought forth, and nourished Christ. She presented him to the Father in the temple, and was united with Him in suffering as He died on the cross. In an utterly singular way she cooperated by her obedience, faith, hope and burning charity in the Saviour's work of restoring divine life to souls. For these reasons Mary is immaculate, all holy, spotless, most highly blessed and ever virgin from her conception, through all her earthly life, death and Assumption into heaven and for all eternity. (Lumen Gentium)*

---

[11] Myendorff, John, *Byzantine Theology*, N.Y. Fordham University Press, 1974, p. 147-148.

Nativity of Mary

Chapter Seven

SECOND EVENT OF THE PRIVATE LIFE OF MARY: HER NATIVITY

MARY'S conception in the womb was a feast of joy of cosmic dimension. It was the dawn of the salvation of the world, and fulfilment of the whole history of the Old Testament.

FEAST OF JOY FOR ALL

HER Nativity was a feast of joy also in the eyes of God, and in the heart of the family of human beings. God had prepared her from all eternity, and humanity could now see with the eyes of the heart the love and concern of God in all its reality. As Mary was a joy since her conception in the womb of Anne, she remained a joy in her birth. "Barrenness" was no longer a shame or a curse because, barren as they were, Joachim and Anne produced the source of life, who would produce the Giver of life, Christ our God. They were like a parched land that bloomed into a garden of paradise, and like a rose that burst open from a rock. The pure happiness that we have expressed at Mary's conception in the womb of Anne becomes at her birth an overflowing river of joy covering again the whole universe.

Everything that is good in creation rushes onward to develop beyond itself into divine beauty. Mary, the new light, comes into darkness, and darkness recognizes her radiance and is illumined by it. Joy is here again the theme of the whole feast as it was in her conception. It is a joy for humanity, for the parents Joachim and Anne, and for the universe.

> *Today glad tidings*
> *go forth to the whole world.*

*Today sweet fragrance
is wafted forth
by the proclamation of salvation.*

*Today is the end of the barrenness
of our nature,
because the barren one becomes a mother.*

*Anne becomes the mother of Mary,
who even after she gave birth,
remained ever-virgin.*

*Mary, the daughter of Anne,
will become the mother
of the One who by His nature
is the Creator and God.*

*He it is who took from Mary his flesh
by which he brought salvation
to the lost.*

*He, the Christ, the Lover of every human being,
and Saviour of our souls. (At Vespers)*

Joy For the Parents

The joy of the Nativity of Mary belongs, naturally, first to Joachim and Anne who, after long years of hope and expectation, of disappointment and social rejection because they were sterile and childless, can now suckle and fondle a child of their own flesh. Now they can enjoy the fruit of their long years of faithful and persevering love for each other:

*Through your holy nativity, O Immaculate One,
Joachim and Anne
were delivered from the shame
of childlessness,
And Adam and Eve
from the corruption of death.*

*Your people, redeemed from the debt of their sins,
cry out to you to honour your birth:*

> *"The barren one gives birth*
> *to the Mother of God,*
> *the Sustainer of our life!"*

We sing again:

> *Today Anne the barren one*
> *claps her hands for joy,*
> *the earth is bathed in light,*
> *Kings sing their happiness,*
> *Priests enjoy all blessings,*
> *and the whole universe rejoices....*
>
> *Behold, no woman will ever again*
> *bear a child in sorrow or anxiety,*
> *for joy has come forth in abundance*
> *and life has filled the world.*
>
> *Joachim's offerings shall no more be rejected,*
> *for the tears of Anne have now been*
> *turned into joy.*
>
> *And Anne can say:*
> *"Rejoice with me,*
> *all you chosen ones of Israel,*
> *for the Lord has given me the palace*
> *of divine and living glory,*
> *to be a place of joy and happiness*
> *for the whole universe*
> *and for the salvation of our souls."*
> *(At the Apostichon)*

From the hearts of Joachim and Anne, joy springs in abundance. It overflows even to their ancestors Jesse and David. David was chosen by God to be the King of Israel and ancestor of Christ. His Kingdom waned and disappeared. Yet "from his roots will grow the branch, Mary, from whom will bloom the flower, Christ, whose Kingdom will endure forever." (Liturgy of Nativity)

Joy for Mary Herself

The liturgy takes a singular pleasure in dwelling on the idea that Christ will come forth from this new child. Even as a baby,

Mary can be called the book in which God the Father has written his "Word." She is "the vine laden with a divine cluster, source of all sweetness." She is the joy of God the Father! Through the whole Office runs a special invitation to angels and to every human being—be jubilant, because the nativity of Mary has erased all sadness of the past:

> *O Virgin, today you were born*
> *a most noble child, from Joachim and Anne....*
>
> *To God you are a heaven, a throne,*
> *and a vase of holiness.*
> *To the whole world, a herald of joy,*
> *the cause of life and blessing.*
> *Through you the curse was wiped out.*
>
> *You are the reason for all the blessings of God.*
>
> *O Maiden, whom God has chosen,*
> *on this day of your nativity*
> *obtain peace and great mercy*
> *for our souls.*

The Office sings again:

> *All you faithful, make haste!*
> *Come to the Mother of God!*
>
> *This is the day of the Lord,*
> *rejoice, therefore, O nations!*
>
> *Behold,*
> *The chamber of light,*
> *the scroll of the Living Word,*
> *has come forth from the womb.*
>
> *The gate that opens to the Rising Sun,*
> *and is ready for the entrance of the High Priest,*
> *is here today.*
>
> *She is the only one who introduced Christ*
> *and Christ alone*
> *into this world,*
> *for the salvation of our souls.*

More than any one else the joy of the feast belongs to Mary herself:

> *Rejoice, O temple of God!*
> *Rejoice, holy mountain!*
> *Rejoice, divine table!*
> *Rejoice, luminous chamber!*
>
> *Rejoice O Mary!*
>
> *Rejoice, Mother of Christ our God!*
> *Rejoice, O immaculate!*
> *Rejoice, O throne of saving fire!*
> *Rejoice, O flaming bush!*
> *Rejoice, O hope of us all!*

THE NAME OF MARY

IN the Old Law a name was officially given a boy on the eighth day of his birth, at his circumcision. So, our Lord was given a name on the eight day of His birth when He was circumcised. A girl was given a name on the very day of her birth.

A name is not a convenient label bestowed upon a person to distinguish him or her from another. The name represents the person. It represents and reveals the person because it enshrines the qualities and attributes of the person. The name describes the person's role in life, and his or her spiritual destiny. A Christian name given to the baptized witnesses to the unusual depth of character of the saint after whom he or she was named, the saint becoming thus the model and ideal to follow.

In the Old Testament, as well as in the New, persons who were called to play a role in the history of salvation received their names by an inspiration from heaven. "Adam and Eve," "Abraham," who had been "Abram" before given his new vocation in life, "John" the Baptist, whose name was given to Zechariah by the angel Gabriel, "Peter" formerly "Simon," "Paul" formerly "Saul," and many others received their name from God when they received a new vocation in life. Our Redeemer Himself was given a name by heaven. The name represents the very person; Holy Scripture "equates" the name with the person. Thus the "Name of God" is identified with God

Himself. Saying the name of a person is dealing with the person himself as present and real. "Hallowed be thy name," "Do not take the name of the Lord, thy God in vain," and "Blessed be the name of the Lord" refer to God Himself.

According to the proto-Evangelium of Saint James, the angel of the Lord who announced to Joachim and Anne gave the order to call her "Miriam," Mary. This name was rarely used in the Old Testament. It appears only one other time. It was the name of the sister of Moses and Aaron (Ex. 15:20-21). The Jewish people seem to have avoided giving this name to their children, as they avoided the names of Abraham, Isaac, Jacob, Moses and Aaron, due to a pious reverence for these great heroes. A similar sentiment prevented Christians from calling their children by the name "Jesus." Early Christians would not use the name of "Mary" either. At the time of Christ, Jewish people started using these names, to honour their children, and perhaps, because of their expectation of the Emmanuel, the Christ, soon to come.

The name Mary means "hope," because Miriam, the sister of Moses, was the "hope" of the liberation which was the promise of God to his people. Exodus says that:

> *Miriam was standing afar off, and taking notice of what would be done to her baby brother lying in the basket. Now Pharaoh's daughter went down to bathe in the river.... Among the reeds she noticed the basket, and she sent her maid to fetch it. She opened it and looked, and saw a baby boy crying; and she was sorry for him.... Then the child's sister said to the Pharaoh's daughter, "Shall I go and find you a nurse among the Hebrew women to suckle the child for you?" "Yes, go," Pharaoh's daughter said to her. (Exodus 2:4-8).*

Miriam saved Moses who would become the saviour of her people Israel. The Fathers and early writers interpreted the name Miriam to mean "the enlightened one," "the light giver," "the exalted one," or simply, "the Lady." Saint Bernard finds another meaning to the name—for him it means "Star of the Sea."

In the Western Church there was a special feast in honour of the name of Mary, on September 12. This feast may well have developed as a consequence of the simple and tender love of the faithful of the Western Church. Saint Bernard's effusive words on the name of Mary may well have further fostered that devotion. Saint Bernard writes:

It is said: "And the Virgin's name was Mary." Let us speak a few words upon this name, which signifies "Star of the Sea." Mary, I say, is a clear and shining star, twinkling with excellencies, and resplendent with example, needfully set to look down upon the surface of this great and wide sea.

O you whosoever you are, you know yourself to be here not so much walking upon firm ground as battered to and fro by the gales and storms of this life's ocean. If you would be not overwhelmed by the tempest, keep your eye fixed upon this star's clear shining. If the hurricanes of temptation rise against you or you are running upon the rocks of trouble, look to the star, call on Mary.

If the waves of pride, or ambition, or slander, or envy toss you, look to the star, call on Mary.

If the billows of anger, or avarice, or the enticements of the flesh beat against your soul's bark, look to Mary.

If the enormity of your sins troubles you, if the foulness of your conscience confounds you, if the dread of judgement appals you, if you begin to slip into the deep of despondency, into the pit of despair, think of Mary....

If you keep her in mind, you will never wander. If she holds you, you will never fall. If she leads you, you will never be weary. If she helps you, you will reach home at last—and so you will prove in yourself how meetly it is said, "and the virgin's name was Mary."
(2nd Nocturne)

HISTORY OF THE FEAST OF THE NATIVITY OF MARY

JUST as the feast of the Dormition of Mary ends the liturgical year, her nativity introduces a new liturgical year. The Nativity of Mary is one of the oldest feasts in the Church. An ancient Palestinian tradition reports that Helen (330), mother of Emperor Constantine the Great, built a church in Jerusalem in honour of the Nativity of Mary. It stood beside a grotto which is today the Church of Saint Anne, kept with great veneration since the second century.[12] Patriarch Anatolios (458), Stephan of Jerusalem of the sixth century, Andrew of Crete, Patriarch Sergius of the seventh century, John of Damascus of the eighth century, and many other poets and hymnographers, wrote beautiful hymns to celebrate the feast.

The Church of the East celebrated it on the eighth of September, nine months less one day, from her conception in her mother's womb which was celebrated on the ninth of the preceding December. From the East, the feast found its way to Rome in the seventh century; later it spread to the whole Western Church. On the day that follows the Nativity of Mary the Eastern Church celebrates the memory of Joachim and Anne, the parents of Mary:

> *Come, O you who love the feast,*
> *let us rejoice, singing,*
> *and let us fervently honour*
> *the memory of Joachim and Anne,*
> *the honourable couple.*
>
> *They have given birth to the Mother of God,*
> *the virgin most pure.*
>
> *O Blessed couple, you have surpassed*
> *all parents in glory,*
> *for you have given birth*
> *to the most beautiful of all the creatures.*
>
> *Truly blessed are you, O Joachim,*
> *because father of the virgin.*
> *Blessed is your womb, O Anne,*
> *for you have brought forth*
> *the mother of our life.*

---

[12] Clemens Kopp, *Itineraires Evangeliques*, translated from German by A. Balkin, Maine, 1963, p. 526.

*Blessed are you who nursed
the one who will nourish him
who nourishes all creation.*

*Therefore, we implore you,
O blessed Joachim and Anne,
to pray to him for the salvation
of our souls.*

The East has a special devotion to Anne as grandmother of our Lord. In Jerusalem and Constantinople, and throughout the whole East, churches were built in her honour. Besides her feast on December 9, the Church has another on July 25. It is the day of her translation into heaven. The West learned of this devotion for Anne, and Rome adopted the feast in the eighth century. From Rome the feast spread throughout Europe in the middle ages, and the feast of Saint Anne became as popular in the West as it was and still is in the East. Every Office of the Byzantine Church and every public prayer ends by remembering first our Lord and God, Jesus Christ, then his Immaculate and all pure mother and his life-giving Cross, and immediately after these remembrances we mention his grandparents Joachim and Anne. They are always present and never forgotten in our official prayers.

Anne and her husband Joachim cared for Mary and raised her with utmost tenderness until the day came to present her "to the Lord in the Temple."

Presentation of Mary

Chapter Eight

THIRD EVENT OF THE PRIVATE LIFE OF MARY: HER ENTRANCE INTO THE TEMPLE OR PRESENTATION

OUR religion's ultimate purpose is to rejoice in life and in the works God has wrought on behalf of our humanity. Our divinization is the first and last aim of God, since *from his heart* we came to be; *in his heart* we abide in security and joy; *to his heart* we shall all return. This is the marvel of all marvels. All other marvels are but an echo and parenthesis in this greater discourse of how a human being can enter into union with Divinity!!! In this event, narrated by miraculous tales, we see our Lady as the model for our own divinization.

THE TALE

CONCERNING Mary, the miracle is not simply the marvellous circumstances in which her parents Joachim and Anne conceived her, nor her glorious birth, nor even the legends with which our imagination surrounds the events of her Dormition and Assumption into heaven. The main aim of our telling these stories is to bring out the miracle of God's love for our humanity shown through her and in her. How is it possible that the Infinite of the Infinite draws a creature, a person of our race, so close and so near to his divine Essence as to make her his mother? The miracle of all miracles is that God dwells in the womb of a girl of this world, and starts human life as a foetus, growing, developing like all of us, and maturing throughout the whole gamut of our human life. All the other details with which we surround these events are but a sudden glimpse of an astonishing underlying reality. They are only a background humming of delight and ecstacy. We marvel and we stammer out expressions of appreciation only to nourish our humanity with the security of God's love. We make up stories and legends, and tell epic tales to bring out the vastness of his undertakings, as a consolation for the sorrows of this world and a demonstration that in the world of God every beauty is possible and true. This is nowhere more true than in the tale of the entry of our Lady into the Temple.

THE ENCHANTMENT OF TALES

In order to communicate the marvels of God's love and of his faithfulness to his creation, our Lord Jesus Christ used legends, gestures and lovely stories. He purposely constructed them to induce us to think, wonder and thus enter into contemplation of the mysteries with ease and joy. The tales, or parables of the Gospels are of course, only one facet of a truth incalculably rich, yet finite only because the capacity of man for whom it has been done is finite.[13]

Christians followed the lead of their heart and tried to imitate their divine Master. In order to communicate the full meaning of the miracles of God's love, they presented them in feasts and in celebrations and wrapped them in poetic hymnography, surrounded by rainbows of sensations, feelings and the heart's affections. Thus the conception of Mary in the womb of Anne was a feast garlanded with solemn rites and stories full of wonder and joy. The poetry displayed at her birth was marked with a flurry of imagination that raised its meaning to the highest power of affirmation and made us cherish it with affectionate remembrance. Witnesses at her nativity are said to have seen new galaxies being born in the heavens, new music sung and a new light shining in the skies. Our traditions concerning the Presentation of Mary are just as moving and awesome as are the earlier events in her life. At the telling of these marvels our hearts instinctively react with songs of praise and admiration.

---

[13] *The Tolkien Reader*, Ballantine Books, New York, p.71.

FROM THE TENT OF GOD TO THE TEMPLE OF GOD

WHEN it comes to translating the extraordinary fact of God's dwelling in a physical place on earth and of being contained in the womb of a girl of our human race, Christians turned to the Old Testament where God was eager to find a place on earth for himself to inhabit and live among his people. He ordered Moses to build him a tent or tabernacle, according to precise details he himself specified. Moses also had to consecrate every object and every furnishing by a solemn anointing with oil in sign and symbol as belonging to God alone for his exclusive use and service. As God said:

> *Anoint the altar of holocaust*
> *with all its furnishings;*
> *and consecrate the altar*
> *which henceforth will be a*
> *most holy thing. (Exodus 40:10)*

Within a simple tent "the glory of God filled the Tabernacle," says the Bible. In this tent, Moses and his people could approach God, talk to him and worship him. It was merely a tent, not a permanent dwelling place.

Five hundred years after Moses, when King David conquered Jerusalem, he made it the capital of his Kingdom. There he dreamed of building a permanent Temple for God to dwell in. He said to Nathan the prophet:

> *Here I am living in a palace of cedar*
> *while the Ark of God dwells in a tent.*
> *(2 Samuel 7:2)*

He gathered money and the best of materials for his son Solomon to build a permanent dwelling place for God. In the year 1000 B.C., the four hundred and eightieth year after the Israelites came out of the land of Egypt (I Kings 6:1), Solomon built a magnificent Temple considered to be the holiest place in Israel, where God resided and around which his glory hovered.

In his ardent prayer at the dedication of the Temple, Solomon poured out all the wisdom of his soul to tell what the temple really meant and what its function was in regard to the relationship of God and his people. He said to God:

> *Why, the heavens and their heavens of heavens*
> *cannot contain You!*
> *How much less this house*
> *that I have built....*
>
> *Day and night let your eyes*
> *watch over this house,*
> *over this place of which*
> *you have said,*
> *"My name shall be there"....*
>
> *When your people Israel are defeated...*
> *if they return to you*
> *and entreat you in this Temple,*
> *hear from heaven!*
>
> *If they repent from their sins*
> *stretching out their hands*
> *towards this Temple,*
> *forgive and act....*   (1 Kings 8:27-40)

In sign of acceptance Yahweh said to Solomon:

> *I grant your prayer and entreaty*
> *I consecrate this house*
> *I place my name there for ever.*
>
> *My heart and my eyes*
> *shall be always there.* (1 Kings 9:3)

Not long after the erection of the Temple, Israel sinned against God and would not repent. God sent the Babylonians to destroy their Temple and take them away into exile and slavery. Among them in exile was the great prophet Ezekiel who preached God's forgiveness and Israel's return to grace. He announced also the restoration of the Temple to a more glorious state than the Temple of Solomon. We read this as prophecy by Ezekiel of the feast of Mary's presentation. The prophecy is made of loveliness, wherein Mary's virginity is described as a closed garden reserved only to the King. There only God resides in beauty and glory and no one else can enter. The Church and all Christianity saw in the description of this new Temple the figure of Mary, the real Temple of God:

> *God Yahweh brought me back*
> *to the outer east gate of the Sanctuary.*
> *It was shut.*
>
> *Yahweh said to me,*
> *"This gate will be kept shut.*
> *No one will open it*
> *or go through it,*
> *Since God has been through it.*
>
> *And so it must be kept shut.*
>
> *The Prince himself, however,*
> *may sit there to take his meal*
> *in the presence of Yahweh.*
>
> *He is to enter and leave*
> *through the porch of the gate."*
> *(Ezekiel 44:1-3)*

What an enchanting metaphor of the ever-virginity of Mary who became the living temple, where the King resides, and where he delights to be among his new people. Mary conceived by the operation of the Holy Spirit, she gave birth in virginity, and she remained a virgin for ever and ever.

THE STORY OF THE ENTRANCE OF MARY INTO THE TEMPLE

THE venerable tradition passed on by her family was that at three years of age, when Mary was ready to awaken to an awareness of social life, she asked her parents Joachim and Anne to present her to the Temple of God in order to prepare herself for the awesome role she was to play in this world. Her parents agreed and brought her to the Temple as an offering and as a precious gift of thanks for the goodness of the Lord to them.

Around this event Christians developed a celebration that only hearts aflame with love for the Lord Jesus Christ, her Son, could imagine and produce. They surrounded it with dignity and solemnity, in order to bring out its meaning, and show their infinite respect for Mary to the Lord. They told the event not simply as historians reporting a fact, but as troubadours of beauty and love. Their imagination soared beyond the confines of human limitations, and introduced humanity to a new order of things where our insight is sharpened and our sensibility purified. We are totally convinced that Mary's supreme dignity as future Bearer of God merits her not only to enter the Temple but to penetrate to the most sacred place of the Temple, the "Holy of Holies." This part of the temple is called the "Holy of Holies" because it contained the "Shekhina," the glory of God, with the Manna, the Rod of Aaron, and the Tablets of the Ten Commandments. Mary was no mere receptacle of signs and symbols, as was the Temple. She was more sacred and holier because she was to contain Glory Himself, the One whom nothing can contain, the God of all:

> *The holy one, the all-blameless one,*
> *moved by the Holy Spirit,*
> *enters the Holy of Holies,*
> *to be fed by an angel.*
>
> *She will become a most holy Temple*
> *to our most Holy God,*
> *Who by dwelling in her,*
> *sanctified the whole creation*
> *and divinized our fallen nature.*
> *(Office of the Feast)*

When Mary entered the temple she was accompanied by all her little friends. Some said that her parents had invited all the girls of the neighbourhood, and some others had heard that the invitation went out to all the girls of Jerusalem. But as it turned out, the whole city walked before Mary with lighted torches. As soon as they reached the court of the temple, Mary alone, unhesitatingly, and with firm determination, went up the steps of the sanctuary where she was to remain in study and contemplation. Not only Jerusalem was ready now to receive God. The whole universe became alive and stood at attention and silence when Mary entered the Temple.

Mary was conceived holy. She was born a joy to God, to her parents and to the whole universe. Now she enters the Temple to prepare herself to become a worthy dwelling place for the Most High. She is the Queen because she is destined to be the Mother of the King of all.

The liturgy describes this Entrance with hymns rich in poetic expressions and dogmatic majesty:

> *Heaven and earth rejoice together today*
> *at the sight of the mystical heaven, Mary.*
>
> *The virgin and immaculate*
> *is entering the holy Temple*
> *to be brought up in honour.*
>
> *Zachary, the high priest,*
> *had this to say to her:*
> *"O Door of the Lord,*
> *to you I open the doors of the Temple.*
>
> *Enter with joy,*
> *for I know and I believe*
> *that salvation will come from you,*
> *and from you will be born*
> *the Word of God."*

Being holier than the angels and more glorious than all the Archangels, Mary was received in a way befitting her dignity and rank:

> *When Anne (this name means grace)*
> *was graced with the pure and ever-virgin Mary,*
> *She presented her to the Temple of God.*
> *She called all her little companions*
> *to carry flaming torches*
> *and walk before her.*
>
> *And she said:*
> *"Go, my child,*
> *to the One Who sent you to me,*
> *for you are promised to him.*
>
> *You are an incense of delicate fragrance.*
> *Enter into the veiled places*
> *and learn the mysteries of God.*

> *Prepare yourself to be*
> *a delightful dwelling place,*
> *for the Lord who grants*
> *great mercy to the world."*

In the Office Mary is constantly called "temple of God," "chosen temple," "temple animated by God and full of his splendours," "temple of the Great King," and "temple broader than the heavens." Hymnographers cannot find any more splendid comparison for Mary entering the temple than being "The Temple of God":

> *O Faithful, let us exchange*
> *glad tidings today,*
> *singing psalms to the Lord,*
> *and hymns in honour*
> *of Mary his Mother.*
>
> *She is his holy Tabernacle,*
> *the Ark that contained the Word*
> *whom nothing can contain.*
>
> *She is offered to God as a child*
> *in a marvellous way.*
>
> *And Zachary, the high priest,*
> *receives her with great joy,*
> *for she is the Dwelling place*
> *of the Most High.*

Thus Mary is a subject of joy, and of admiration and love. God is pleased at the sight of a beautiful little girl surrendering to a way of life which is a mystery even to herself. She walks straight to meet the high priest who is filled with joy at her sight. Angels "admire and rejoice," and Joachim and Anne forget their sorrow and overcome the breaking of their heart to look at her "with fullness of joy."

Hymnographers insist that in all truthfulness, Mary is the "palace of the King of glory," the "palace of the Wisdom of God." She is also the "tabernacle sacred and celestial." The Kontakion summarizes this flurry of comparisons by declaring:

The most pure Temple of the Saviour,
his most precious bridal chamber,

the little girl of our humanity,
sacred treasury of God's glory,

enters today into the house of the Lord,
bringing with her the grace of the Holy Spirit.

Wherefore the angels of God are singing
"Behold the heavenly Tabernacle."

EDUCATION OF MARY

AT that time, while there were schools for boys in Israel, there was no provision for the education of girls. The majority of rabbis were hostile to female education. Accordingly, if a girl acquired the arts of reading and writing, she did so at home under the guidance of her father or mother, or anyone who had schooling and formal education.

Christians deemed it worthy of God to arrange a very special system of schooling for Mary, a system full of enchantment and challenge. Some said that Mary's tutor was the high priest, Zachary himself, and some others added that angels came down from heaven to supplement the high priest's religious education with the arts and crafts. So Mary acquired a familiarity not only with the contents of religion and the messianic prophecies but also with arts and sciences of her time. She was also trained in all the finest literary works of poetry and all human niceties of social life. She was formed to be a perfect Lady.

God willed all these extraordinary measures to prepare Mary to be his Mother. He had chosen her from all eternity and now He was calling her to answer his expectations for perfection. Generously and willingly, Mary answered the invitation and entered the Temple not only to become the perfect exemplary of womanhood but also to be the perfect human educator of our Lord. Is it not because she was a perfect teacher that the Gospel says that the Lord "grew to maturity and he was filled with wisdom"? And again, "he increased in stature and in favour before God and men (Luke 2:40,52)." After all the care Mary received in the Temple, she really became the perfect Woman in body and soul.

Every Jew was encouraged to pray often. A Jew was expected to begin and end the day in prayer; grace was said before and after meals; psalms were recommended for private recitation; every contingency of life was to be met by suitable prayer. We love to imagine Mary excelling in understanding and in practicing all the high ideals of her Jewish religion and attaining the highest degree of freedom in mystic prayer.

Her years of preparation in the Temple made her a perfect creature in every endeavour and in every virtue. Humanity feels at ease in presenting her to God as a Mother full of dignity and clarity. We human beings try to match his generosity and goodness with a generosity and goodness of our own namely by presenting him with the best product of our human race who would become his Blessed Mother.

ICON OF THE FEAST

THIS is a typical icon, reproduced in innumerable forms by all Christian cultures, Western and Eastern.

A three year old child, Mary, is dressed in the flowing robes of a grown up woman. Even as a child she is aware of what is happening. She is hastening to the temple, the tip of her toes barely touching the ground. Her three companions are right behind her with intense looks centred on her, while she is lifting up her hands to the welcoming hands of the high priest Zachary, who is waiting, tall and majestic, at the door.

Joachim and Anne can hardly keep up with their hastening child. Joachim stands tall, rather sad for his little girl's departure. Anne also seems sad and powerless. Yet she looks right into the eyes of her husband, to console him and probably to explain.

Every detail of this icon breathes determination and clarity. Joy is coming down from heaven and springing from the earth. The movements of the personages are more dramatic than is generally permitted in icons. In the upper right corner, on top of the tower of the temple, Mary is again represented being served food by the Archangel Gabriel. The swooping angel with finely spread wings, the heavy awning fastened to the top of the tower of the city, and the projecting bough of some dark tree, are signs that heaven and earth, nature itself, angels and men, are fully conscious to receive the good news and to celebrate together the

Presentation of Mary

astounding actions of both God and humanity. We too, the onlookers, cannot help but be transfixed and inspired with joy and pride in our Lady the Theotokos, coming as a child to the Temple and being herself, the very Temple of God.

Chapter Nine

FOURTH EVENT OF THE PRIVATE LIFE OF MARY: HER DORMITION–ASSUMPTION

HOLY Scripture does not say anything about the death and Assumption of Mary. The last mention of her in the New Testament is in the Acts of the Apostles. After the Ascension of the Lord into heaven, the Apostles returned

> *to Jerusalem...and when they reached the city they went to the upper room where they were staying.... They joined in continuous prayer, together with several women, including Mary the mother of Jesus.... (Acts 1:12-14)*

We do not know exactly how long Mary lived after that event or where she spent the rest of her life. But her family and contemporaries who lived with her kept alive the memory of some details of her life and especially those of her death and Assumption. They told them to their children and to their children's children. Eastern people are faithful to family traditions which they treasure and carefully transmit to posterity. Thus traditions ceaselessly unite one generation with another. The bare facts remain clear and constant but the details develop over time, becoming brighter and more striking, in the same way as life develops.

HISTORY OF THE FEAST

CHRISTIANS hesitated at first to give names to such extraordinary events as her Dormition and Assumption. They called them respectively *Koimesis* (sleep) or *Dormition*, and *Analepsis* or translation. The word *Koimesis* (Dormition) connotes two distinct, yet inseparable events. One is Mary's death, and the other is her resurrection which was followed by her Assumption into heaven. The word Assumption or Translation carries a passive connotation. It suggests that Mary went up into heaven not by her own power, but by the power of another. This is the central difference between "Assumption" and the word "Ascension" which is applied to the Lord. Our Lord ascended by his own power because he was God; thus, His going up was called "Ascension." Mary did not ascend—she was "assumed," taken up and carried up to heaven; her ascent is therefore called "Assumption."

The death and Assumption of Mary are facts of history. But the time and place and the circumstances surrounding them are not exactly known. Some think they happened in the year Fifty in Jerusalem; some others say they took place later, at Ephesus, where Mary was believed to have lived in the care of the Evangelist and beloved disciple of the Lord, John. But most Eastern writers and the whole Office of the Byzantine Church assert that she died in Jerusalem. The Apostles were all present at her death to bid her farewell. Saint Thomas, who was in India, came three days later. When the Apostles took him down to Gethsemane where they had deposited her they found only a hip of perfumed flowers in her coffin. An angel of the Lord told them of her resurrection and Assumption at the hands of her Son.

The first and most explicit writer who relates this Palestinian tradition is Bishop Meliton who lived in the fourth century. He tells a story long existing in his diocese, which must have been told by Peter, James and John, the three disciples who were privileged to witness the Transfiguration of the Lord on Mount Tabor. These same apostles were also privileged to witness the death and burial of Mary. Meliton says:

> *After she died*
> *the disciples deposited her on a stretcher*
> *and asked one another who will be the one*
> *who will carry the palm frond*
> *at the head of the procession.*

And Meliton goes on with a special delight to tell the old story circulating in his diocese. He writes:

*John said to Peter:
"Since you preside
over us, you deserve to carry it."*

*Peter answered:
"I would rather carry the body."*

*James said:
"Since I am the last of the Apostles,
I will carry it with you, O Peter!"*

*They were of one accord
and John carried the palm.*

*Beholding the stretcher
high above their heads,
Peter and James intoned psalm 113:
"When Israel came out of Egypt...
Judah became his sanctuary
and Israel his domain...."*

*In the name of the other Apostles
and of all the people present, Peter said:
"O our Lord,
it would be fitting and right for you
to raise the body of your own mother,
and to lead her to the joy of heaven,
as you saw fit and right
to choose her to be your mother."*

*The Lord answered him and said:
"Let it be according to your wish!"*

*And the Lord Jesus raised
his mother from the dead.
Angels and archangels came down from heaven
and carried her into the heavens....*

Inspired by this delightful story the liturgy sings:

*O Virgin Mother of God,
At your Dormition was present
James, the first bishop of Jerusalem,
and brother of the Lord.*

> *So were Peter, the honoured
> leader of the Apostles,
> and Paul, the preacher of the Gentiles,
> together with the sacred
> company of the Apostles.*
>
> *They sang praises in honour
> of the divine and amazing mystery
> of the working of Christ our God,
> and they rejoiced.*
>
> *They buried your body,
> the Source of Life and Temple of God.*
>
> *On high the angelic Powers
> bowed in wonder
> before this marvel.*
>
> *They said to one another:
> "Lift up your gates
> and receive the one
> who bore the Creator
> of heaven and earth."*

Besides Meliton another ecclesiastical writer of the sixth century, Theoteknos, Bishop of Livias on the Left Bank of the Jordan river (550-560), tells also of a very old tradition that was still alive in his church describing the death and Assumption of Mary. He relates this event in this way:

> *If the God-bearing body of Mary has known death,
> it has not suffered corruption.*
>
> *It has been preserved from corruption
> and kept free from stain.*
>
> *And it has been raised to heaven
> with her pure spotless soul
> by the holy angels and the powers of heaven.*

Later in his sermon he adds:

> *It was fitting that the most holy body of Mary,
> The God-bearing body, receptacle of God,
> divinized, incorruptible and illuminated*

> *by divine grace and full of glory,*
> *should be entrusted to the earth for a little while.*
>
> *It was raised up to heaven in glory*
> *with her soul pleasing to God. (Wenger, l'Assumption)*

The Patriarch of Alexandria, Theodosius (566), reflects on a dual celebration popular in Egypt in his time. One is the feast of Mary's death on January 16, and the other her resurrection and assumption on the 9th of August. He thus allowed a delay of two hundred and six days between the two events. As to whether our Lady's body during this time was corrupt or incorrupt, Theodosius does not say. But he asserts that the two facts are certain and well known and celebrated everywhere in Egypt.

In the year 600, Emperor Mauricius (582-602) decreed that the Death and Assumption of Mary be celebrated on the 15th of August in Constantinople, the capital of the empire. Shortly thereafter, Ireland was the first church in the West to adopt the feast, and just fifty years later it was introduced into Rome. Pope Sergius (687-701) mentions that at his time it was known and celebrated in his diocese of Rome. By the eighth century it was celebrated everywhere in both East and West.

Saint Andrew of Crete (720), who was originally from Jerusalem and consequently familiar with the local traditions of his Church, Saint Germanus of Constantinople (733), and Saint John of Damascus, all gave lengthy homilies extolling the Death and Assumption of Mary.

In his sermon on the Dormition of Mary, Patriarch Modestus of Jerusalem (634) tells the story of Christ coming down from heaven in the presence of his apostles to assist his Mother, together with them, in the hour of her death. He says that as she was held in the arms of her Son:

> *Mary trembled with love and excitement,*
> *and her soul flew to meet him.*

And he adds:

> *But, in order*
> *to make her share*
> *in the incorruptibility of his own body*
> *he attracted her*

in a way he alone knows how...
And took her up to heaven with him....

Modestus repeats once more in the same sermon the bare facts of the Death and Assumption as they had been handed down by the tradition of his church. He was anxious to ward off strange tales and interpretations which some Christian factions were adding to propagate heretical teachings. Blinded by folkloric propensity, some people of his time were melding facts and strange customs into an inextricable muddle. The Church has always been fearful of condoning such distortions. The bare facts are marvellous enough in themselves. All they need is a tale of glory, a framework of beauty worthy of the truth they contain. To justify our wonder and amazement at the workings of God in favour of our humanity, we need only a delicate touch of the inspiration of artists, and the imagination of poets to weave a frame of thrill and of delight around the bare facts.

God's marvellous choice of Mary as his Mother, and the fact that a girl of our humanity became the Bearer of God, comprised the "stuff" that inflamed the heart and imagination of Christians and led them to tell tales of enchantment and delight. Unseen wonders became visible realities, and impossible events became facts. This happened for each of the four main events in the life of Mary the Theotokos!

At the *conception* of Mary in the womb of Anne her mother, all sorts of voices were heard in the heavens and on earth.

At her *birth* all kinds of miracles were told. The laws of nature were said to have been changed in favour of a sterile couple, Joachim and Anne, who suddenly became fertile and alive to procreate a child Mary long after they reached old age.

The *Temple,* which was closed to all females, *opened its doors* to receive the one destined to become the Mother of God. Angels were seen serving her and always present to her needs. The great high priest himself was her teacher and mentor.

Finally at her *death*, clouds formed in the heavens, and magic carpets transported the Apostles from the four corners of the earth to Jerusalem to pay their last tributes to the one who gave birth to the Lord of all. At Vespers we sing the story in all the eight tones:

*The Holy apostles were taken up
from every corner of the world,
and carried upon clouds by order of God.*

*And they gathered around your pure remains,
O Source of Life, and kissed them with reverence.*

*As for the most sublime Powers of heaven,
they came with their own Leader,
To escort and to pay their last respects
to the most honourable body
that had contained Life Itself.*

*Filled with awe, they marched
together with the Apostles in silent majesty,
professing to the Princes of heaven
in a hushed voice:
"Behold, the Queen of all,
the divine maiden is coming!"*

*Lift up your gates and receive
with becoming majesty
the Mother of the Light that never fades.*

*Because through her,
salvation was made possible for our human race.*

*She is the one upon whom no one may gaze,
and to whom no one is able
to render sufficient glory.*

*For the special honour
that made her sublime is beyond our understanding.*

*Wherefore, O most pure Mother of God,
forever alive with your Son,
the Source of Life,
do not cease to intercede with Him,
that He may guard and save your people
from every trouble,
for you are our intercessor.*

*To you we sing a hymn of glory
with loud and joyful voices, now and forever.*
                    (At Vespers)

This story does not attempt to scale the heights of God, but only to satisfy our desire to understand his truth, which is more marvellous than all the marvels we can imagine or desire. The workings of God are, indeed, beyond human expectations. They demand daring imagination to describe them or relate them.

In her association with God, Mary unites the finite and the Infinite, the temporal and the Eternal. Fallen humanity is transformed into a new creation, and the carnal into the spiritual. God descends to become human without ceasing to be God, and the human ascends to divinization, without ceasing to be human.

This is the marvel of God's love!
This is the wonder of God's working!

Thus stories, tales, and epic poetry have to go on. They capture the kind of relationship that binds humanity to God and God to humanity. So great is the beauty with which the human person has been treated that he may now dare to guess that in some kind of joyful fantasy he may actually assist in the riches of God's creation.

MEANING OF THE FEAST

DORMITION does not commemorate Mary's death as such, but what life-after-death really is, and what entry into the Kingdom means. Dormition refers to the one who is alive, who is at home, who has actually arrived at her goal on the other side of death. She has entered into "life-to-come," and our human nature is wholly fulfilled in her body and soul. Mary is the supreme success and masterpiece of the work of God in our humanity.

Entering "life-to-come" is not exactly a dying, but a new becoming; it is a bursting forth of life that casts off decay and leaves behind disintegration once and for all. It is a becoming and a pure beginning. The celebration of Dormition really means that from death comes only life and not decay. Mary is the sign of things to come: the sign of the Kingdom of God already come, the sign of the creation already saved, and the sign of the life to come where God is "all in all" (Col.3:11).

In celebrating death, Christians do not give any thought to surrendering the old self; we rather revel in the ultimate validation of life, affirming the resurrection of all and the final outcome of our life, which is eternal glory. Mary was mortal, like all mortals. She died, and her death was a passage from an apparent defeat of our human nature to triumph, from an apparent end of hope to fullness of life. She is the representative of renewed humanity, the New Eve, who introduced human nature into a new perspective of life, as the first Eve introduced it to sin and misery.

Death-Dormition-Assumption is a Christian trilogy celebrating the final victory of Christ in the Mother of God and ultimately, the final victory of our human nature over corruption and darkness, wherein the whole human being enters into salvation. Undiminished, we fuse into God who preserves our uniqueness and our personality whole.

More than any other feast of Mary, the Dormition is dogmatic in nature. It insists on the truth of the two natures of Christ, who is true God and true man and the divinization of creation and of humanity. Jesus Christ, Son of God, God of God, was in our human nature as perfect a man as he was in the Trinity a perfect God. He was the son of Mary, and Mary was his real Mother, more Mother to him than any mother is to her child. His human reality was taken from her very flesh and blood, and from her alone, the substance of all humanity.

Divine Worth of the Human Person

In his Incarnation, God the Son received a human body in the womb of Mary His Mother, and He became one with us. In his body, He thought and prayed, loved, and worked out our redemption. In this same body He experienced the whole gamut of life. Finally, in his body, he entered the darkness of the tomb to rise again and ascend into glory. Christ was God. Corruption had no dominion over him. He rose glorious from the tomb because he was God. He raised His body to the throne of heaven because in His body He was still God of God:

> *Christ...having been raised from the dead, will never die again. Death has no power over Him any more...so, His life now is life with God.*
> *(Rom.6:9-10)*

Christ is the ultimate reality of every human person. As He has risen and seated Himself at the right hand of the Father in glory, so also will every human person rise and ascend to glory in Him and because of Him. This is shown in the Dormition-Assumption of Mary. She is the prototype of our humanity, redeemed and saved. This is the clear teaching of our religion. When God the Father revealed His son, He revealed also His infinite love for humanity:

> *God so loved the world*
> *that He gave his only son.*
> *so that every one who believed in him*
> *may not be lost*
> *but may have eternal life. (John 3:16)*

The end and destiny of the human person is, therefore, plenitude of life, plenitude of glory, and infinite beatitude in God. The on-going process of human development, of conception and birth, of struggling and growing, of declining and dying, will be crowned and shown in all its divine glory. Saint Paul sings again, "Christ will transfigure these wretched bodies of ours into copies of his glorious body (Phil. 3:21)."

Long before the Parousia, Christ shared his incorruptibility with the one who shared with Him her corruptible nature. He made her body a copy of His glorious Resurrection. Mary died and was buried as every human person. But her Son raised her from the dead before the end of time. He commanded angels to carry her into the heavens. Mary, therefore, is the preview of humanity's final triumph, and the exemplary of that "life to come" which we proclaim to be a doctrine of our belief.

In her Death-Resurrection-Assumption Mary recovered the sublime reality of the perfect "image and resemblance of God" as it was designed by God and given to our first parents. She is the paradigm of all human beings who will recover in Christ the original innocence of creation.

This state of final triumph had been seen by Job:

> *This I know: that my Redeemer lives....*
> *After my awakening, He will set me close to Him,*
> *and from my flesh I shall look on God.*

> *He whom I shall see will take my part.*
> *These eyes will gaze on Him and find Him not aloof.*
> *(Job 19:25-27)*

In Christ, and because of our divinization in him, despair and pessimism have no more reason to exist. Humiliation of decomposition and stench will be avenged and replaced by glory and brilliance. Therefore, artificiality and cynicism have no more foothold in human life—they are transformed into harmony and perfect equilibrium.

In the dignity of such a woman, Mary, we can also fully understand the immeasurable dignity of womanhood and the grandeur of the female person. Here we experience, as a fact, that womanhood's dignity is as lofty as the dignity that is in the manhood of Christ. As Christ ascended into the heavens to fill the universe with His own divine presence as man, so also Mary, as woman, was assumed into the same heavens to fill them with the glory of femininity. In the Mother of God, the female person appears to be what God intended her to be, a hymn of glory and exultation.

Saint Paul speaks of our baptism as a way of identification with Christ:

> *God, who is rich in mercy, loved us with a great love. Even when we were dead in sins, he quickened us together with Christ, and raised us up together, and made us sit together in heaven in Christ Jesus.*
> *(Eph. 2:4-6)*

According to Paul, baptism is a participation in Christ's resurrection and ascension. By sharing her whole being with the Lord, Mary participates in a much greater closeness and similarity with her Son than even with baptism. Christ is of one substance with the Father and is forever one with the Godhead; He is of one human nature with his Mother and is forever united with her, and through her with every human person and with creation. As her divine Son protected her integrity as virgin and as mother, he also saved her body from the corruption of death.

Every human being receives half of his human reality from his mother and half from his father. Christ received his whole humanity from his mother alone. Because of this special identification of Mother and Son we conclude that it would not be to the honour of the Son to permit corruption and disintegration to touch his mother's flesh. This would be an insult to his very Person, and a defeat of his work of redemption and divinization.

The Resurrection and Assumption of Mary after death were the only fitting conclusions to her life on earth as we sing in the liturgy:

> *Death and the tomb could not*
> *retain the Mother of God....*
>
> *Since she is the Mother of Life*
> *You lifted her up to life.*
>
> *O You, who have dwelt*
> *in her ever virginal womb.*

The liturgy does not cease singing:

> *O marvellous wonder!*
>
> *The Source of Life is laid in the tomb*
> *and the tomb becomes a ladder to heaven!*
> *Rejoice, therefore, O Gethsemane,*
> *Sacred abode of the Mother of God!*

LITURGY OF THE DORMITION–ASSUMPTION

THE celebration of the Dormition-Assumption of Mary is overwhelming with expressions of triumph and joy. The angels rejoice at having their queen entering the Kingdom. The Son of God rejoices on seeing his mother restored to glory and the liturgy creates around all the events a biblical atmosphere. It seeks to link the New Testament to the Old, and the Old to the New. Old and New Testaments are not divided, much less opposed—the first is the prototype of the second.

At the Dormition-Assumption of Mary we chant hymns recalling the story of the Burning Bush where God's presence was a real fire that penetrated a whole dried up bush, yet did not consume it. This is the prototype of Mary holding God in her body and yet not overcome by the glory of his divinity. Mary was like the "Ark of the Covenant" that carried God from the desert to the promised land. She was also the "Garden of Paradise" that held in its midst the Tree of life, Christ our God.

At Vespers we read the story of "Jacob's Ladder" that united heaven to earth. The ladder of Jacob was well established on earth while touching the highest heaven. The corresponding miracle is that Mary remained a girl of our human race, one of us, a real child of Joachim and Anne, while carrying heaven and bringing humanity and earth up to heaven.

We read also the prophecy of Ezekiel where we recognize Mary as the gate of the chamber which no one dares penetrate but the Prince, Christ God, who became man in her (Ez.44:1-3). And finally, in the book of Proverbs, we recognize her as the "seat of the Wisdom of God" (Prov. 9:1-6), and the receptacle of divinity.

A hymn at Lauds tells us that the Apostles who witnessed the Ascension of the Lord were all present to witness the Assumption of his mother. In Christ's Ascension they witnessed his Godhead; in Mary's Assumption they saw the return of humanity to the heart of God, its Source and its Origin.

In her Dormition-Assumption, Mary becomes the first fruit of our humanity to enter body and soul into eternal glory. Her body, which was "made larger than the heavens by containing the One whom nothing can contain," is elevated to fill the universe with salvation and brilliance. Christ's tomb was the place of resurrection. Mary's tomb was the gate to Assumption. In her, humanity finds a source of glad tidings and proof of the faithfulness of God. Death is no longer a separation but a step towards perfect union with him.

Destiny of the Human Body

The liturgy insists on the glorification of "the august and holy body of Mary," the one that contained God and by which we were divinized. The number of hymns that sing of and glorify her body makes the Dormition appear as a special celebration for the human body as well and also for the matter of this universe. Both are destined to be transfigured and are already being transfigured into the glory of the Son of God.

Innumerable hymns whisper sentiments of sadness and praise the tears of the apostles shed for their separation from a beloved figure, but the acclamations of joy and triumph are more numerous yet, extolling her triumph and the happy ending of her life. The whole Office is an uninterrupted hymn declaring that it was impossible that the Mother of Life, Jesus Christ who is our Life and our very Lord and God, would be submitted to the humiliation of final annihilation while her flesh and blood was still alive and glorious in her risen Son. The thought of victory of life over death is all-pervading through every hymn of the liturgy:

> *All you peoples, come, let us sing.*
> *The virgins who follow her*
> *shall be brought to the King.*
> *With gladness and rejoicing*
> *they shall be brought to him.*
>
> *She through whom*
> *we have been made divine,*
> *is indeed of the seed of David.*
>
> *Gloriously and ineffable*
> *she recommends herself*
> *into the hands of her own Son and Master.*
>
> *Praising her as the Bearer of our God*
> *we cry out and say,*
> *"We confess that you are Bearer of God.*
>
> *Save us from all distress*
> *and grant our souls deliverance*
> *from all tribulations."*

Every event of the life of Mary is celebrated as a superb interplay between the laws of nature and the laws of God, who delights in creating new laws in honour of his mother. In her he showed what he intended humanity to be, and what it shall be one day—a glory and a perfect harmony of delight.

Paraclisis

There is a liturgical office called *Paraclisis* or prayer of consolation. It is recited or solemnly chanted during the fifteen days preceding the celebration of the Dormition-Assumption of Mary on August 15. As the Acathist hymn is the prayer extolling the glory of divinization of humanity, the Paraclisis is the prayer of sighing and groaning over our misery and sin. In paraclisis we enumerate all the evils and aches and pains of life. The prayer describes the diseases of our body and soul, of wars and natural disasters that beset us every day of our life. We cry to the Mother of the Lord that we are crucified "on a bed of suffering." We find no help, nor consolation sure and forthcoming but in her. She is Mother of mercy and source of healing.

The prayer does not mention or explain the origin or reason for these ills. They are facts of our daily life. If there is a reason for evil it is not in the past but in the future. After evil and death there is resurrection. After sin and suffering there is the brilliance of the face of God. Mary is the perfect example and paradigm of our own life. In life, she encountered ecstasy and joy and suffered the pain of His crucifixion and death with her Son. She encountered death and separation and she passed to Resurrection. After death she entered beatitude.

This is the real end of our history, the achievement of our existence. Our choice, our faith, the purpose of all our struggles and our only goal is God.

Almost two thousand years ago Saint Paul declared that all pain and sorrow will be absorbed by Resurrection. All is empty discourse if we do not talk about Resurrection and see that Resurrection is the final outcome of all sadness. God seems sometimes hidden, discretely watching our miseries but he really is the One coming. He is the One who attracts us, and reveals himself to us in final Resurrection!

As a conclusion to the Office of Paraclisis we pray:

Gracious Virgin, victory will come to those who put their trust in the strength of your arm, for we sinners who stoop with the weight of our sins have none before God to plead for us but you.

- O Mother of God most high, we bend our knee to you: deliver your faithful servants from every kind of trouble.

- You are joy to the distressed, you are strength to the oppressed, you are food to those who sink into despair.

- You console all the strangers, you support all the blind, and you come and visit all the sick. You are shelter to

the weary, you are comfort to the crushed, you are heavenly assistance to the orphans.

- You are the Mother of God most high, and so we pray to you: hasten, O immaculate one, and save your faithful servants!

- In you is all my hope, O Mother of God: place me under the wings of your protection.

Beginning of the Liturgical Year

The Eastern Church starts the liturgical year in September by commemorating the birth of Mary. She closes it in the last month of the year, the month of August with her Dormition. While maintaining January first as the beginning of the civil year as it was established by Julius Augustus Caesar, the Council of Nicea (325) ordered the Church calendar to start on September 1.

On that date the Roman Empire commemorated the victory of Constantine the Great over Maxentius. The Church commemorated it also, and added the celebration of her liberation and her civil freedom. It was fitting, indeed, to celebrate at the same time the heralding of the salvation of mankind and liberation from the slavery of sin by the birth of the Mother of God.

Your Nativity, O Mother of God, was a herald of joy to the universe.

From you rose the Sun of Justice, Christ our God.

He cancelled the curse and poured forth his grace.

He vanquished death, and granted us eternal life.

To close the liturgical year the Church instituted the death and Assumption of Mary. At her death, men and angels combine their liturgical prayer in a synergy to celebrate the final victory of humanity and its glorious entering into the Kingdom of God.

O our Sovereign, by an all-powerful divine injunction

*The chorus of theologians
from all the corners of the earth*

*And the multitude of angels
from above, in heaven,*

*Run to Sion to officiate
in a worthy way*

*At the deposition of your Body
in the tomb!*

The liturgical time for the commemoration of Dormition-Assumption is the longest of all the commemorations of our Lady. The first fifteen days of the month is a period of strict abstinence. Every day we chant the Office of Paraclisis.

Before we see our Lady enter the Kingdom in complete triumph and fullness of life, we remember all our miseries of life, our temptations, our sins, and the moral and physical defeats which submerge us. We ask for help, guidance, strength and consolation. The celebration is very solemn and extends almost to the end of the month when we start preparing for the celebration of her Nativity to begin the new liturgical year.

ICON OF THE DORMITION

IN this icon, the Apostles are assembled around the body of Mary, all in a position expressing sadness and sorrow. They were brought on clouds, as on magic carpets, to Jerusalem by angels from all the corners of the earth. Angels and Apostles are shown in the upper part of the icon.

In the lower part, St. Paul is on the right bowing low to the Mother of the Lord. On the left, Peter is swinging a censor in honour of the body that bore the Lord.

In the back stand three figures in Bishop's vestments recognizable by the omophoria with large crosses. They are, on the left, Dionysius the Aeropagite with one cross showing, and John of Damascus with two crosses. On the right, behind the Apostles, stands Andrew of Crete. In their writings, these three gave all the details of the legends that surround the facts of the Dormition-Assumption of Mary.

Christ stands behind the bier, between two candlesticks, holding the soul of his mother in his hands. Above him, in the upper centre, two angels are carrying her up to heaven. This is the Assumption of the soul which forms a special type in icon painting of the Dormition.

Thus, we see in theology, liturgy, and iconography the central truths and the legends and tales of the major events of the life of our Lady the Theotokos. These sublime melodies have been composed for us to sing with our hearts and our lives the generous love of Almighty God for our humanity. They direct our eyes and our attention beyond our daily ills and miseries to our glorious destiny—and help us to realize the divine worth of our human person:

> *Today rivers of blessings*
> *flow upon creation.*
> *O heaven, rejoice together with the angels!*
> *O you creation of God, rejoice!*

The Dormition

Part Three

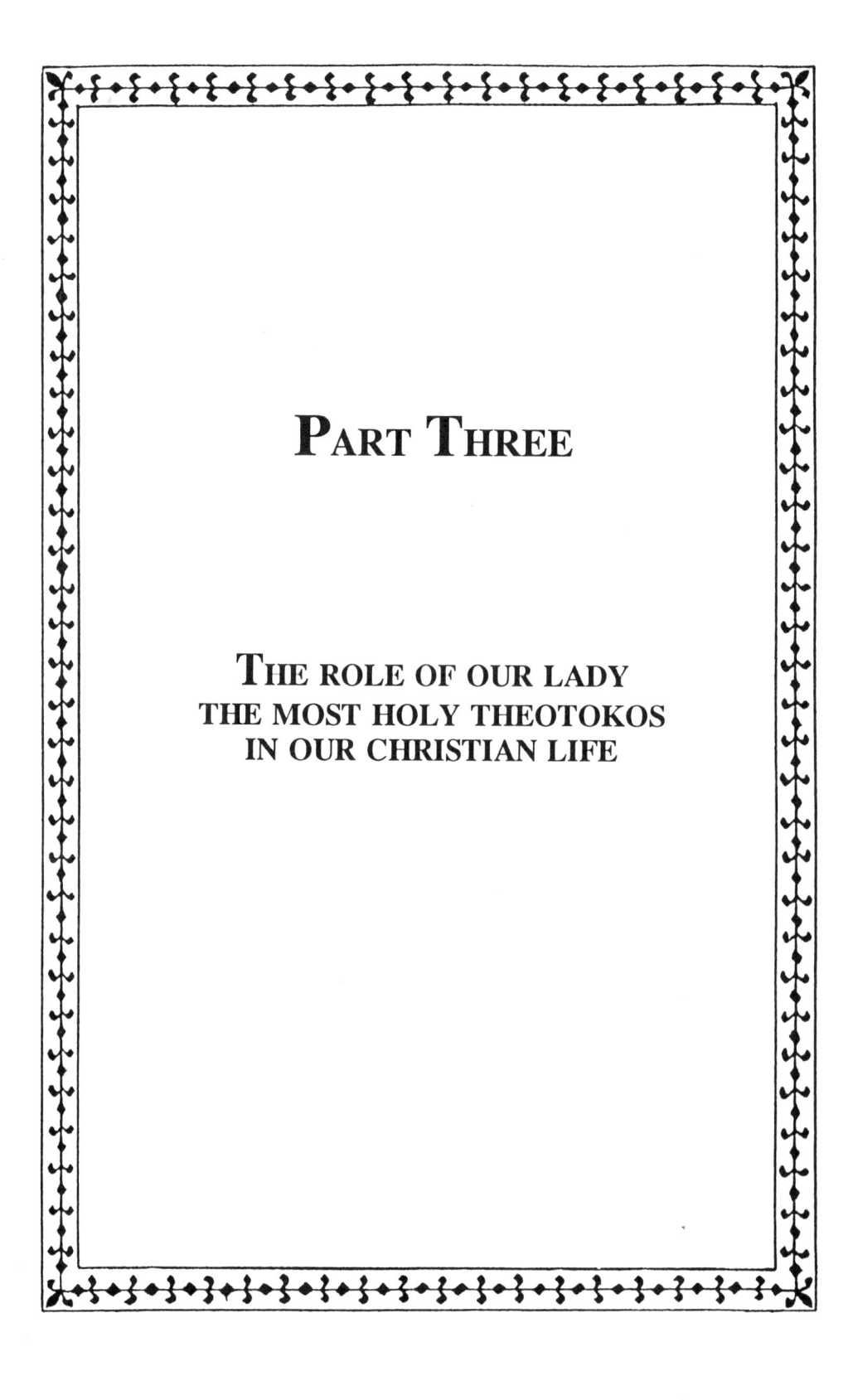

The role of our lady the most holy theotokos in our christian life

Chapter Ten

THE ROLE OF MARY IN OUR CHRISTIAN LIFE

MARY IN THE EARLY CHRISTIAN COMMUNITY

THROUGHOUT the public life of her Son, Mary kept in the background. After her Son had gone to heaven she seems to have provided leadership until the Holy Spirit came down. She appears to have been the focal point of the assembly. All ancient icons of Pentecost show her in the midst of the Apostles as the rallying force of unification to prepare for the reception of the Holy Spirit. In the book of Acts she is shown present in the Upper Room as the earthly and visible heart of the Church (Acts 1:14). After the descent of the Holy Spirit, she resumes her unassuming role of silence, prayer and contemplative love.

A HISTORY OF HONOURING OUR LADY

FOR a long time Christians refrained from any expression exalting her other than "Mother of the Lord." Later in history they talked about her glories, but not as favours that were granted to her arbitrarily which would set her apart from the rest of humanity. Rather, her supereminent gifts and graces were always related to her being the Mother of the Lord. Saint Augustine affirms that she was "clearly the mother of us all...since she co-operated out of love, so that there might be born in the church the faithful who are members of Christ, their head."[14] It is this careful attitude of always relating Mary to the Incarnation which

---

[14] Saint Augustine, *De S. Virginitate*.

has created an admirable balance in the expression of Christians' outlook on her role in our life.

Devotion to Mary does not make her the centre of our religion, but only an accompaniment to the symphony which is Christ. Whatever we say about Mary must come from Christ and be only a background whisper to his music. It is only at the side of her Son that Mary presides over the destinies of the world. Any exaggeration or pietistic sentimentality about her, any literary platitude or small talk of sensibility, would be mere infantile curiosity. Such aberrations can disrupt the harmony that God is displaying in our salvation, and the integrity of the meaning of the Incarnation. Balance and harmony are necessary in all our ways of expressing devotion to the Theotokos.

In the Liturgy

For fear of upsetting this balance the liturgy urges us to be discrete in expressing fantasies and impossible situations to make Mary seem unreal. In the ninth Ode of the Canon of Christmas, we are warned to be sober in speaking about her:

> *O you who combined Virginity and Motherhood,*
> *it is perplexing to sing your praises.*
>
> *We should prefer to be silent.*
> *Silence is easier and safer.*
>
> *But the surge of love that burns in us*
> *compels us to sing your glory.*
>
> *O Mother, grant us the ability*
> *to meet the immense desire*
> *that draws us to sing your praise.*

The Ancient Church considered that dogmatic definitions about Mary were not proper because definitions would tend to make of her a superhuman creature, a creature from another world, which would be an attack on the simple reality of the Incarnation. But once they simply realized that she had handled and suckled the Eternal One, they started proclaiming her and ascribing to her supreme beauty, grace and dignity. Even angels stand in awe before her.

We speak about Mary only in relation to her Son, and we draw conclusions based upon this relation. In her, God the Word became really human without any loss of his divinity. In her he acquired a human intelligence and a human will, while remaining the Wisdom of God and the all-infinite Creator who made everything out of nothing. Consequently, if queens are glorious, Mary is more glorious than glory. If mothers are tender and loving, Mary is the essence of tenderness and love. She is the Mother of the most loving King, and of the King of all Kings. She is therefore Queen of us all. Because her very flesh and blood became God's flesh and blood, we sing to her the most sublime of hymns, and the mere breath of her becomes life-giving for all humanity:

*I shall open my mouth
and it will be filled with the Spirit.*

*I will break forth into a hymn of glory
to the Mother and Queen.*

*With great joy I will present myself to honour her
and sing her glories with exultation. (Acathist hymn)*

In Preaching

The Council of Ephesus produced a tremendous devotion to Mary through steady preaching, especially on the occasion of her feasts. Most of these sermons followed the same pattern:

They first recalled the fall of man and the contrast between Mary and Eve;
then they developed the scene of the Annunciation;
and they ended with the birth of Christ.

The sermons were lavishly adorned with Old Testament texts applied to Mary. The prototype of such sermons was delivered by Theodotus of Ancyra who died in 440. He delivered his sermon on the occasion of the feast of the Purification of Mary and the Presentation of our Lord into the Temple which happened to fall on the same day as the Council of Ephesus. Theodotus, as all other contemporary preachers, taught that Mary was really purified, not by her obedience to the Law of Moses but "through the

Incarnation." She was "burned pure" through the approach of the divine and immaterial fire of the Godhead, so that henceforth she remained inaccessible to sin.

It is thought also that Theodotus introduced on that occasion a new style in preaching. He used the greeting of the archangel to Mary in a string of salutations which became standard in expressing love, devotion and admiration to the Mother of God. He started his sermon by these salutations:

> *Rejoice, you whom we have so long desired.*
> *Rejoice, brightness of the church.*
> *Rejoice, spiritual fleece of salvation.*
> *Rejoice, stainless Mother of holiness.*

This type of preaching became popular in the Byzantine Church throughout the following centuries.[15]

In Pilgrimages and Lighting Candles

Beside the sermons and homilies pronounced in honour of Mary in which the Churches of East and West expressed their devotion and love to her, they used also material signs and symbols.

It is through signs and symbols that human persons enter into relationship with the invisible. It is through signs and symbols that they can express the deepest realities of their human souls. We human beings need signs and symbols as props to bolster our attention and sustain our fervour in the presence of the invisible.

Among some of the most important signs of our devotion to the Blessed Mother of God are the construction of shrines to our Lady, walking in pilgrimages to her shrines, and the lighting of candles in front of her icons.

Walking in pilgrimages evokes the image of the restless, wandering human heart, which cannot find repose until tired of wandering, finally coming to rest close to God who dwells in the very being of Mary. The journey which our heart cannot or will not make has thus to be undertaken by the body, in an endlessly

---

[15] G.G. Meersseman, *Hymn of the Acathist*.

repeated gesture. It is important to put the body to work to overcome the unwillingness of the heart.

The candle's flame is also a symbol of the desire of our soul to be always alive and attentive to God. Nothing in nature is more alive and more attentive than a flame. A flame flickers and dances at the most delicate touch of air, breath or movement.

When it is left quietly burning in front of an icon after we have departed, it keeps dissolving itself in warmth and delight. We leave the candle behind because by ourselves we feel incapable of surrendering completely to the will of God. The candle is more responsive to God's touch and more malleable than the living heart of man:

> *In our human longing we walk in pilgrimage and we light the willing candle as signs of our inner eagerness to reach God and to be always present and alive at his touch.*[16]

SPECIAL SIGNS OF DEVOTION IN THE WESTERN CHURCH

THE Churches of East and West well realized the awesomeness of Mary who has been brought so close to the Divine Essence that the very God of all has dwelt in her womb and is identified with her as her Son! They understood also that since Mary's conception in the womb of her mother Anne, Mary must have been the object of the good pleasure of God the Father. Her whole life was a growth into the splendour of grace and virtue until her death. We can follow her progress, step by step, from her total submission to God at the Annunciation, where she became his vessel of holiness, until her death and final glorification in her Assumption.

To remember the events of the life of Christ and of his mother and relive their meaning in one's own life, Western Christians use the rosary in a special way, recalling to mind the fifteen main events, or "mysteries," of the life of Christ our God, and of Mary his Mother. The mention of these events precedes the *Our Father*, followed by a decade of *Hail Mary's* and concluded

---

[16] Schillebeeck, *Mary, Mother of Redemption*, 1955.

by the *Glory be to the Father and to the Son and to the Holy Spirit....*

There are also special signs of devotion in listening to locutions or voices from heaven, and in honouring apparitions of Mary or even of Our Lord Himself carrying a special message to humanity. The places of such apparitions become centres of pilgrimage open to all those who hunger and thirst for spiritual realities. In these shrines miracles might happen. God can, indeed, pierce the clouds of our human hesitations and unbelief by sending a bright note of his glory, a "miracle" that points to the Parousia.

Innumerable other practices of devotion to the Mother of God are widespread, including special prayers (novenas) for special intentions, consecrations and dedications of one's own life to Mary, and particular acts of charity to attain holiness. There are also many hymns in praise of Mary and of her Son, and many official and scientific writings including encyclicals of popes and letters of saints.

DEVOTION TO MARY IN THE EASTERN CHURCH

THE depth of the concern God has shown in his Incarnation, and the love for humanity he has demonstrated in choosing a girl of our race to be his Mother on earth, expand our heart and mind to the dimensions of the sublime and the miraculous. God's workings in Mary help us to understand and appreciate his love. We express it in songs of praise, and in liturgies of pure delight. Saints, poets and artists combine their genius to sing about the intoxication of their souls in hymns and epics of divine beauty. Their theme is not the human being, not Mary, but God and the marvel of his condescension in Mary. Mary is the ground or humus for his activity and the radiance of his grandeur.

Innumerable are the poets and hymnographers who used the typology of the Old Testament, and applied it in a loving and admiring way to the Mother of God. One of the most known Church hymnographers and poets is Romanos the Melodist, called "The Hymnographer" (490-560). In a special poem he wrote on the occasion of the Nativity, he makes her say to Christ her Son:

> *I am not simply your Mother.*
> *You have made me also to be*

> *the mouth and the glory of my whole race.*
> *For all humanity I beseech You.*
>
> *In me your world has a mighty protectress,*
> *a wall and a support.*
> *Those who have been exiled*
> *from the paradise of delight*
> *look to me for salvation.*

At the end of the poem he whispers in the name of all:

> *Through her prayers,*
> *who is ever-virgin and Theotokos,*
> *spare me, O Lord.*

THE ACATHIST HYMN

THE most famous poetical work of Romanos in honour of Mary is an Acathist hymn. *Acathist* means a prayer during which people do not sit. The Christian people stand in majesty when addressing God because they are facing Majesty. They do not sit because they are in the presence of the most awesome mystery of God who radiates upon them grandeur and divine worth. They recognize their worth and stand while adoring, praising and singing glory.

Romanos starts his poetical epic on Mary by first applying to her what the Old Testament predicts about her—not in a dry enumeration, but applied to her in a dramatic way. Heaven and earth, angels and humanity, and the whole universe, sing her praises in concert. The episodes of Holy Scripture come back to life before our very eyes, and they set our hearts aflame. We join the chorus of all those who, with Mary, witnessed the Incarnation: Gabriel, Joseph, her cousin Elizabeth, the Magi, Babylon and Egypt, heaven and earth; and those who did not witness the Incarnation but longed to see it, the Prophets and all the saints of the Old Law.

The hymn brings back to our consciousness the reasons why we honour Mary and why we sing to her what we sing: she is Mother of God, a mirror of Christ. She is the bridge between heaven and earth. In her flesh, she carries the Saviour to humanity and humanity to God.

She is "the Salvation of humanity as Moses was of his people." She is the "Manna" who nourishes us with Christ. She is the "Ark that contained the glory of the Lord." She is the "Mystic Mountain" where Moses had a vision of God, and "from which the Cornerstone, Christ, had been cut."

After enumerating the predictions of the Old Testament about Mary, Romanos sings of her maternity. She nourished with her own life Christ our God. As Mother of God her holiness and beauty are such that even angels fall in admiration before her. Her maternity and virginity are miraculous because of the infinite Word of God who was enclosed in her womb. Mary cannot be admired and loved without this concurrent consciousness of God's condescension and love. No prayer expressing love and veneration for Mary can be compared to this hymn.

Literary Composition of the Hymn

The Acathist hymn is composed of a canon of nine Odes and of a kontakion in four parts.

A canon is a lengthy series of short poems, separated into groups under a category called "Odes." "Ode" means a song. In any given Canon there are never more than nine Odes, fashioned after the nine original Odes of Holy Scripture. In our Christian Odes, the second Ode of Scripture is generally omitted because of its threat of vengeance and punishment.

After speaking of the Archangel Gabriel announcing the glad tidings to Mary, the Canon breaks forth in jubilation, and sets the tone for the whole hymn:

> *I will open my mouth*
> *and it shall be filled with the Spirit.*
>
> *I will break forth into a hymn of glory*
> *to the Mother and Queen.*
>
> *With joy I will present myself*
> *to honour her,*
> *and sing her glories with exultation.*

The Canon goes on to salute and praise the Mother of God. Ode after Ode sings her titles as prefigured in the Old Testament and realized in the New, and all this in true Christian style and with a rare sense of fitness. These Odes are rich, breathing forth love, admiration and praise for the immaculate and glorious Lady and the Dawn of our salvation, Christ God.

After the Canon comes the Kontakion. A *Kontakion* was originally a long series of hymns written on a membrane rolled around a short thin piece of wood, hence the name "Kontakion"—short. In reality it was a complete epic poem, a long sermon in poetical form. It appeared in the Church in the 6th century to match in majesty and beauty the soaring dome of Holy Wisdom. The Acathist hymn of Romanos in honour of Mary is the most famous of all the Kontakia of the Church. It is composed of four parts, each part containing six chants. The whole Kontakion thus has twenty-four chants.

The chants are called *Oikoi*, "houses" or "structures," a paradigm to be followed, so that the whole hymn may be a complete unity. They follow each other, as a string of special salutations to the Mother of God. The salutations start with the word "Chaire" which the Archangel used at the time of the Annunciation. This word is generally rendered in English by the word "Hail" as in the prayer "Hail Mary, full of grace." But the word means more than "Hail" or "Hello" or "Good Morning." *Chaire* is a Scriptural word connoting a messianic message and announcing a special intervention of God on behalf of his people. The word "Rejoice" is more fitting.

The chants end by the cry *Chaire, Nymphy anymphevte,* which means "Rejoice, O Spouse no man can ever claim for a wife," rendered in English by "Rejoice, O Bride and Maiden ever virgin."

After the long chant comes a shorter one which contains a narrative episode of a special action of God, a message that elucidates a face of the Incarnation. It always ends with a cry of admiration and amazement, the word "Alleluia!"

The whole Kontakion has a magnificent preamble summarizing the idea of the Incarnation:

> *As soon as the angel had received his command,*
> *he hastened to Joseph's house*
> *and said to the ever-virginal one:*
> *"Behold, heaven was brought down to earth*
> *when the Word Himself*

was fully contained in you!
Now that I see Him in your womb,
taking a servant's form,
I cry out to you in wonder:
Rejoice O Bride and Maiden ever-pure!"

Following are some excerpts from this Kontakion.

First Part: Annunciation and Incarnation

The first part describes the scene of the Annunciation by the archangel, his conversation with Mary, her final acceptance of God's invitation, and her complete surrender to his will. It tells also of her visit to her cousin Elizabeth, of Joseph's doubts, and of his joy when he finally understood that Mary conceived through the action of the Holy Spirit.

First Chant

An archangel was sent from heaven to greet the Mother of God. And as he saw you taking a body, O Lord, at the sound of his bodiless voice, he stood rapt in amazement and cried out to her in these words:

Rejoice, O you through whom joy will shine forth;
Rejoice, O you through whom the curse will vanish!

Rejoice, O Restoration of the fallen Adam;
Rejoice, O Redemption of the tears of Eve!

Rejoice O peak above the reach of human logic;
Rejoice, O depth beyond the sight of angels!

Rejoice O you who have become a kingly throne;
Rejoice, O you who carry Him who carries the Universe!

Rejoice, O star who manifests the Sun,
Rejoice, O womb of the divine Incarnation!

Rejoice, O you through whom creation is renewed;
Rejoice, O you through whom the Creator becomes a Babe!

—Rejoice, O bride and Maiden ever-virgin!

The Annunciation

Fourth Chant

When the power of the Most High overshadowed the one who had never known the nuptial bed, her fruitful womb conceived, and she became for all the delicious field: for those who wished to reap salvation by singing: Alleluia!

Second Part: The Adoration of the Magi

The second part is composed of six chants also. It recalls the story of the adoration of the shepherds, of the magi and their secret warning by the angel to return to Babylon by another way, announcing to all the coming of Christ. It tells of Christ's flight to Egypt where idols fall and errors are dispelled. On the fortieth day the divine Child is presented to Simeon in the temple, revealing his divinity:

Twelfth Chant

When Simeon was about to leave the present world, You were entrusted to him as an infant, but You revealed Yourself to him to be the perfect God, wherefore he marvelled at your wisdom beyond words, and he cried out: Alleluia!

Third Part: Our Divinization

The six chants of the third part give an account of the new life established by the divine Son of the Virgin. Divinization has been wrought, and the attention of humanity is now directed toward divine happenings. Indeed, Christ came to show us the way to heaven. Heaven is indeed the abode whence he came and which was always present in him while he was on earth. With great wonder angels behold the Son of God taking flesh and abiding on earth. Philosophers and theologians cannot understand or express the marvel of love revealed in this condescension of God. As for us, the faithful, we proclaim and sing it in joy, saying: alleluia!

Fifteenth Chant

While fully present amid those below, the uncircumscribed Word was in no way absent from those above: for what happened was a divine condescension, and not a moving from one place to another; and it was a birth from a virgin inspired by God, who heard these words:

Rejoice, O Space of the spaceless God;
Rejoice, O Gate of the sublime Mystery!
Rejoice, O Message unsure to men without faith;
Rejoice, O glory most certain to those who believe!
Rejoice, O sacred Chariot of the One above the Cherubim;
Rejoice, perfect Dwelling of the One above the Seraphim!
Rejoice, O you who reconciled opposites;
Rejoice O you who combined maidenhood and motherhood!
Rejoice, O you through whom transgression was erased;
Rejoice, O you through whom Paradise was opened!
Rejoice, O Key to the kingdom of Christ;
Rejoice, O Hope for the ages of bliss!

—Rejoice, O Bride and Maiden ever-pure!

Eighteenth Chant

Desiring to save the world, the Creator of all came down to this creation of his own will. Being one of us, our Shepherd and our God, He appeared among us, a man like us. The like called upon the like, but as God He heard us sing: Alleluia!

Fourth Part: Mary, Guide to Christ

The six chants of the fourth part contain invocations and glorious praises of the divine maternity. Mary is Mother of the Creator of all, a unique vessel containing all graces and blessings. She, consequently, stands as a beam of light guiding us all to her Son in whom we find forgiveness and salvation:

Twenty-Third Chant

By singing praises to your Son, we all exalt you as a spiritual temple, O mother of God! For the One who dwelt within your womb, the Lord who holds all things in his hand, sanctified you, glorified you and taught us all to sing to you:

Rejoice, O tabernacle of God the Word;
Rejoice, holy one, holier than all saints.

Rejoice, O ark that the Holy Spirit has gilded;
Rejoice, O inexhaustible treasure of life.

Rejoice, O unshakable tower of the Church,
Rejoice, O impregnable wall of the Kingdom.

Rejoice, O you through whom banners of triumph are raised.
Rejoice, O you through whom enemies are routed.

Rejoice, O healing of my body
Rejoice, O salvation of my soul.

—Rejoice, O bride and Maiden ever-virgin!

And the hymn closes with this prayer full of tenderness and confidence:

> *O Mother worthy of all praise,*
> *You who have given birth to the Word,*
> *the Holiest of all the holy ones,*
> *accept this offering we depose at your feet.*
>
> *Deliver every human being from affliction,*
> *and save from future punishment those*
> *who cry out and sing to you:*
> *Alleluia!*

Kontakion of the Incarnation

I am your own, O Mother of God!
To you, protectress and leader,
my songs of victory!

To you, who saved me from danger,
my hymn of thanksgiving!

In your invincible might,
deliver me from all danger,

> *that I may sing to you:*
> *"Hail, O Bride and Maiden ever-virgin!"*

Conclusion of the Whole Hymn

The whole Office concludes all the praises and songs of glory by this hymn:

> *Gabriel was rapt in amazement as he beheld your virginity and the splendour of your purity, O Mother of God, and he cried out to you: "By what name shall I call you? I am bewildered; I am lost! I shall greet you as I was commanded to do: 'Rejoice, O Woman full of grace!'"*

EPILOGUE

CEASELESSLY we proclaim that Mary's intercession is always powerful and effective; yet we know that her intercession does not dispense us from struggles, suffering, and the effort to co-operate (*synergi*) with the grace of God in order to realize the ideal of Christian life and attain to the Kingdom. We cannot be saved without our own co-operation and free, personal acceptance of the gift of God.

Since salvation is our restoration to the liberty of the children of God, we cannot be saved without free and continual action on our part. In our prayers to be saved by the powerful influence of Mary, we constantly remind ourselves that we have to co-operate in our own redemption:

> *Luminous nuptial Chamber of Christ,*
> *O virgin full of grace,*
> *through your prayers*
> *help us become tabernacles*
> *of God Father-Son-Spirit,*
> *by the co-operation of*
> *our good deeds. (Office of Matins)*

Our devotion to Mary does not acquit us from any part of our involvement with Christ. We should not for one moment imagine that our veneration for Mary is likely to make us lead victoriously

Christian lives by substituting Mary for ourselves. Our liturgical prayers repeat constantly that by ourselves we are hopeless bunglers, doomed to make a mess of everything!

How true this is with all of us. If we think that Mary will do our praying and work for us, and then everything will be all right, we will be heretical. Only when we identify ourselves so completely with Mary's prayer that we deepen our own faith and intensify our own love will we become more courageous and more enthusiastic in working and struggling to do God's will.

Then, everything will indeed be all right. We do not substitute Mary for ourselves. We grow in holiness only if we allow God to penetrate more and more deeply into our souls, and only if our divinization becomes our way of life. Once we are thus existentially committed, we are able to achieve our Christian goals together with Mary and with the power of her love.

Rejoice, O Woman full of grace!